Luther
for
Evangelicals

Luther

for

Evangelicals

A REINTRODUCTION

Paul R. Hinlicky

B

Baker Academic

a division of Baker Publishing Group
Grand Rapids, Michigan

© 2018 by Paul R. Hinlicky

Published by Baker Academic
a division of Baker Publishing Group
PO Box 6287, Grand Rapids, MI 49516-6287
www.bakeracademic.com

Printed and bound by CPI Group (UK) Ltd, Croydon, CR0 4YY

Library of Congress Cataloging-in-Publication Data
Names: Hinlicky, Paul R., author.
Title: Luther for Evangelicals : a reintroduction / Paul R. Hinlicky.
Description: Grand Rapids : Baker Publishing Group, 2018. | Includes bibliographical references.
Identifiers: LCCN 2017055547 | ISBN 9780801098888 (pbk. : alk. paper)
Subjects: LCSH: Luther, Martin, 1483–1546. | Reformed Church—Doctrines. | Evangelicalism.
Classification: LCC BR332.5 .H56 2018 | DDC 230/.41092—dc23
LC record available at https://lccn.loc.gov/2017055547

Unless indicated otherwise, Scripture quotations are from the New Revised Standard Version of the Bible, copyright © 1989, by the Division of Christian Education of the National Council of the Churches of Christ in the United States of America. Used by permission. All rights reserved.

In keeping with biblical principles of creation stewardship, Baker Publishing Group advocates the responsible use of our natural resources. As a member of the Green Press Initiative, our company uses recycled paper when possible. The text paper of this book is composed in part of post-consumer waste.

green
press
INITIATIVE

18 19 20 21 22 23 24   7 6 5 4 3 2 1

For Július Filo and James Mauney,
the bishops in my life, alike evangelicals.

Contents

Contents

Preface

THIS BOOK IS A WORK in theological hermeneutics—not strictly a historical introduction to Luther's theology,[1] but rather an interested introduction addressed to the specific audience of English-speaking evangelicals. As such it is yet another work in my scholarly project of liberating Luther from Lutheranism to make him available as a resource to the rest of the Christian world (naturally, I would like also to liberate contemporary Lutheranism for Luther, but that is another story). This book brings also a certain satisfaction of a personal debt I owe to evangelicalism.

Beginning with a high school drama teacher, Mr. Franklin Harris, my own journey of faith has been enriched and stimulated by American evangelicals. Mr. Harris played for me and my thespian friends a tape recording of a revival at Asbury College, which had the hoped-for effect on me of a new and adult experience of the faith. My brother Mark and I, who sometimes quarreled terribly growing up, subsequently attended a Billy Graham Crusade at Yankee Stadium in New York City and walked, arm in arm, down to the crowd that went forward at the end of the sermon. To this day, I think that the message—if not the sacramental delivery—of Luther's "joyful exchange" has not been better expressed or more widely disseminated in American culture than by Graham's choir singing Charlotte Eliot's hymn "Just As I Am." In time, however, I was made by personal

ambition and academic aspiration to feel somewhat ashamed of these
youthful excesses in revivalism, even though in truth I had flirted also
for a time with the charismatic movement.

But I did not much cotton to the intellectual obscurantism or
petty moralism that I encountered among some evangelicals and
charismatics. My adult discovery of Luther's way came when a seminary professor, John Groh, guided me to reading Luther's polemical
writings against Karlstadt, Müntzer, and Zwingli. To be sure, these
polemical writings hardly serve well in a book such as this one, which
is rather more interested in building bridges; they are necessary
reading, but for those already matriculated in Luther studies. All
the same, I would be lying if I denied that reorganization of affects
that evangelicals call the "new birth," which came home to me, a
believer since my baptism as an infant, in those tumultuous times of
emergence from adolescence to adulthood in the 1960s. This book
is a personal acknowledgment of that debt to evangelicalism and a
small effort to satisfy it. For that formative experience informs my
reading of Luther's doctrine of faith, as that exposition is unfolded
in the following pages. Be it noted that my reading is in some tension with the standard doctrine of Lutheranism from the 1580 Book
of Concord, which separated justifying faith and regeneration into
two different things.

I am also grateful to my Roanoke College colleague of seventeen
years, Gerald R. McDermott, who through countless conversations
taught me much about the history and dynamics of evangelicalism.
He offered valuable commentary on the opening portion of this book.
Likewise I am grateful to Robert Benne, whose personal engagement
with evangelicals is far greater than my own, and to my newer colleague James Peterson, who cautioned against the insensitive usage
of habitual in-house Lutheran lingo that would be offensive to my
target audience. Offenses that remain are entirely the responsibility
of this author! I would also like to thank Gordon Isaac of Gordon-
Conwell Theological Seminary for his sympathetic reading of the
manuscript and his encouragement, especially with regard to the
pertinence of the intervention I make in this book. Finally, thanks

are due to Ms. Cara Anderson, my research assistant at Roanoke College, who helped with proofing and indexing.

I try in what follows to win over evangelicals to a fresh reading of Luther, well grounded in the current changes in direction taking place in the field.[2] I aim to convince them to undertake the theological task of reading Luther for themselves, freed from some influential but misleading interpretive clichés. My strategy is to discuss lesser-known writings and in the process to clear up at least some of the perceived obstacles to evangelical reappropriation today of the theology of the sixteenth-century reformer, taken as a teaching theologian, not a hero or prophet (or for that matter, a villain). The scholarly arguments for my more controversial statements about Luther's theology in debate with other scholars, accordingly, do not appear much in this volume. Those interested should consult my other books, as they are referenced in the endnotes. I have likewise tried to keep the scholarly apparatus to a bare minimum. The purpose is to provoke readers to look at Luther and see for themselves. Of course, along the way I try to provide reasons why this resourcing in Luther is needed today and beneficial—namely, the account of the "crisis" in evangelical theology that is laid out in the introduction and further elaborated at the beginning of part 2.

This book is dedicated to two bishops who in the course of my life and ministry have "overseen" me in ways personal, pastoral, and evangelical. Július Filo was my mentor for my family's sojourn in Slovakia in the 1990s. A product of Lutheran Pietism, but also an intellectual forged in the fire of Dubček's crushed Prague Spring, Filo always lifted up "faith operative in love" as the holistic mission of the post-Christendom church. I matured to an adult knowledge of my ancestral Slovak language while listening to his beautiful intonation of the liturgy and his existentially gripping sermons, suffused always with his own warm piety.

James Mauney has been my bishop for the eighteen years since we left Slovakia in 1999 and came to Roanoke College. I know of no bishop today who is a more passionate proclaimer of the crucified and risen Lord. He welcomed me and sustained pastoral friendship with me through thick and thin—no easy task in the case of the prickly personality who is your present author! Much of the material in the present book is adapted from studies in Luther that Mauney commissioned me to write for the pastors of our synod in preparation for the five hundredth anniversary of the Reformation. I am happily in his debt and salute his episcopal "mission accomplished" on the occasion of his retirement.

Paul R. Hinlicky
Easter 2017

Introduction

MARTIN LUTHER needs to be reintroduced to the evangelical theological world. This is true today for a number of reasons. First and foremost, Luther is not the possession of the denominations named after him. Historically speaking, Lutheranism is Luther as mediated by his younger colleague, Philipp Melanchthon, who survived him and put a decisive but ultimately misleading cast on his legacy. The resulting Lutheranism from the beginning dove into "identity politics," accentuating certain kinds of differences from other Christians while ignoring certain kinds of affinities. Luther, to be sure, battled as much with would-be allies as with declared enemies. This embattled Luther, certain of the impending end of days, was henceforth pressed into service, made over into the prophetic founder of Lutheranism, which thought of itself as the true, visible church of God on earth. Other Christians ever since have taken Luther as filtered by the various Lutheran representations of him (as prophet, as hero of individual conscience, as national liberator, and always as enemy of all things Roman)—even as these others were also caught up in identity politics of their own. In recent times, however, a new Luther picture is emerging that conscientiously seeks to identify and avoid such fallacies.[1]

Second, evangelical theology needs a fresh introduction to Luther because Luther is one of its neglected but significant theological sources.

If, historically, we see the sources of evangelicalism in the Puritan doctrine of the new birth descending from Calvinist Anglicanism, the Wesleyan doctrine of the new birth descending from Arminianism, and the Anabaptist doctrine of the new birth as conformation to the cross and resurrection of Christ, we can in different ways trace these genealogies back to Luther's doctrine of justification by faith. By the same token, these various sources of evangelicalism are not entirely compatible with each other; indeed, in some ways they militate against each other and can coexist only to the extent that an inarticulate experience of the new birth is elevated over the understanding of it. But that elevation of experience over understanding has had its day. Evangelical theology today is in a state of internal crisis precisely across this axis.

We can by way of introduction orient our project with the help of two recent works: the *Oxford Handbook of Evangelical Theology*, edited by my friend and former colleague Gerald McDermott; and *New York Times* opinion writer and University of North Carolina historian Molly Worthen's history of evangelicalism, *Apostles of Reason*.[2] The *Oxford Handbook* champions the thesis that evangelical theology (as opposed to popular evangelicalism) has come of age, forsaking fundamentalism and ecumenical isolation to grope its way back to the Great Tradition. Worthen's history, on the other hand, argues that evangelicalism in the twentieth century has been the very uneasy alliance of Mennonites, Wesleyans, and Reformed, united in that elevation of the experience of the new birth, to be sure, but intellectually dominated by the rationalistic fundamentalism articulated in the Reformed doctrine of biblical inerrancy.

In different ways, both theses are true. Contemporary evangelical theology cannot any longer sustain the a priori, rationalistic theses that (1) a perfect being must reveal in a perfect scripture, and that (2) this principle of inerrancy comes first and is axiomatic such that (3) those who deny inerrancy can be "othered" as "liberals" not sharing a biblical worldview and so unworthy of theological engagement. But if these lines of intellectual defense fall, as they must today, all that remains to evangelicalism, it seems, is a shared experience of the new birth variously understood.

Yet all is hardly lost. Evangelicalism has preserved precious accents of the gospel as Luther understands it in ways better than other Christians have, even better than many "Lutherans." A renewed understanding of Luther's doctrine of faith can give precise definition to the new birth as dying with Christ and rising in Him to newness of life. Because this new birth is believed on the basis of the word of God, it is experienced; it is not believed because it is experienced (which would be believing in one's own feelings rather than in the word of Christ). Because the word of God is the word concerning Christ, the newborn believer can let the Bible be what it really is: the manger bearing the Child, the chamber pot holding a precious treasure, the Spirit's matrix of the faith-forming word of peace from God through the risen—that is to say, vindicated—Christ. In the luminance of this gospel Word of God, the Bible can be the imperfect, even erring, all-too-human book of many and diverse witnesses that in spite of all, *mirabile dictu*, presents Christ to speak His joyful exchange, "Give me your sins and take my righteousness! Give me your death and take my life!" And because the living Christ who conquered sin and death is present in faith this way, the newborn believer gets to be a Christian not in name only but also in deed, a "little Christ" to every wounded person who appears in her path. Mercifully, the Christian does not ever *have* to show God that she is worthy of grace; being justified by faith, she *has* peace with God! Rather, the newborn Christian *gets* to show God's love in Christ to others, even as she has first been loved.

The preceding paragraph sketches Luther's take on the four characteristic preoccupations of evangelicalism that British scholar David Bebbington lifted up: evangelicalism, he said, can be identified by its emphases on (1) conversion, (2) Scripture, (3) mission, and (4) the cross. And so part 1 of this book is organized into four chapters looking at Luther through the lenses of each of these themes. The purpose of these studies, however, is not to replace reading Luther but rather to invite reading Luther directly. By overcoming characteristic misunderstandings of Luther within conflicted evangelicalism today, this book breaks ground for a renewed encounter with the Luther texts identified.

One of the fateful castings of Luther by Melanchthon, followed by Calvin, was to take Luther more as a prophet than a teacher—a hyperbolic rhetorician or pulpit orator whose way of talking was not to be taken, strictly speaking, as referencing a way of being, as reality. This casting stands behind the cliché that verbose Luther was not a "systematic" thinker. This interpretation of Luther, however, confuses Luther's embattled contextual engagements and variegated employment of genres with Luther's consistent theological substance. As mentioned, the cliché, first fixed by Melanchthon at Luther's funeral oration, was that Luther was like an Old Testament prophet, an unsystematic oracular voice from the Lord whose deliverances were now to be tamed by a "systematic" theology like Melanchthon's own or later Calvin's.

This narrative is deeply misleading. There is a theological coherence to Luther, but it must be found in the creedal and catechetical genres in which he chose to work. Thus Luther's kind of coherence is not that of a closed system of reasoning. Instead, as we shall see, coherence brings Luther to entertain certain kinds of dilemmas, aporias, or conundrums that faith must sustain between the light of grace and the light of glory rather than prematurely resolve, as a closed theological system would press, even require. Part 2 thus provides a re-presentation of Luther's dogmatic theology by way of an interpretive discussion of his own most doctrinally important work, the Large Catechism. Again, the purpose is not to replace reading Luther for oneself with yet another Lutheran interpretation of Luther, but to catalyze a direct encounter with these basic texts of Luther for contemporary evangelicalism in its state of theological crisis after the collapse of the doctrine of biblical inerrancy.

I have made a point of including along the way some of Luther's hymn texts in the recommended reading (the full lyrics of the hymns I discuss are found in the appendix). For here Luther and evangelicalism find common ground in wanting to utilize popular forms of music to evangelize—that is, to sing the gospel into the human heart and in this affective way instruct the human mind. What evangelical theologians may make special note of, however, is that Luther's hymns discuss human experience only in the context of a proclamation of the story of God's way to humanity—never as an independent phenomenon or autonomous source of the knowledge of God.

The outcome of the hoped-for encounter with Luther texts promoted in what follows cannot, I think, be controlled or predicted. We can leave that up to the Spirit! But my presumption is that Luther can help evangelicalism through the present crisis of the collapse of the fundamentalist doctrine of biblical inerrancy by the retrieval of a better understanding of its core claim that justifying faith brings a new organization of affects, a new subjectivity, as Jesus explained the new birth to Nicodemus as a Spirit-wrought birth from above. This better understanding of the new birth, in turn, not only puts Scripture, mission, and cross in new and better light but also points to evangelical mission by the Christian torah, the "method of catechism," as part 2 lays out.

One final accent by way of introduction. Luther, as this book contends, is a witness to Jesus Christ and a teacher of the faith in Him that justifies the sinner; he is not particularly, let alone especially, relevant as a saint, a prophet, or a hero. Indeed, it is to be frankly acknowledged that for some—recalling his treatment of pope, peasant, and Jew—he was (and remains to this day) a villain. There is no need to obfuscate here. Like all of us Christians, Luther was in certain ways a man in contradiction—if indeed he is right that Romans 7, situated between baptism (Rom. 6) and consummation (Rom. 8), describes the *Christian* life. In the case of his larger-than-life personality, his particular self-contradictions (as I will note along the way) are rather dramatically on display in his conflicts with papists and enthusiasts, rabbis and rabble-rousers. Luther the Christian made some bad choices in his life's journey. Like many an academic, he was not particularly well prepared for the rough-and-tumble of politics into which life threw him. In this genuine seesaw struggle of the Spirit against the flesh of the justified sinner, Luther and today's evangelicals (and this author as well!) are on common ground. And that observation about the Christian who never ceases to be in need of a savior from sin leads to our opening overture on Luther's famous hymn "A Mighty Fortress Is Our God."

Overture:
"A Mighty Fortress Is Our God"

L UTHER'S MOST FAMOUS AND BELOVED HYMN is a meditation on Psalm 46.[1] Luther wrote it in the politically tense time between the Peasants' Revolt in 1525 and the Diet at Augsburg in 1530. During this period the threat of martyrdom loomed over him—an important clue to the hymn's meaning. In it Luther retrieves the early Christian theology of the martyrs and what scholars call the "apocalyptic" perspective of New Testament theology.

Brace yourselves! Luther's theology is radical, disruptive, more and more disturbing the better we understand it. With the opening verse Luther situates us in a war going on above us and around us and even within us—a war between good and evil! Scholars call this battle-theology "apocalyptic." It is the biblical genre that arose in Second Temple Judaism, which we see in books such as Daniel and apocryphal literature such as the Dead Sea Scrolls of the Qumran community. Apocalypse literally means "revelation," but in a very specific sense: God unveiling and putting into effect His plan of battle to win back the creation that has fallen prey to the contra-divine powers and principalities of sin, death, and devil.

A mighty fortress is our God,
a bulwark never failing;
our helper he, amid the flood
of mortal ills prevailing.
For still our ancient foe
doth seek to work us woe;
his craft and power are great,
and armed with cruel hate,
on earth is not his equal.

The twentieth-century Lutheran theologian and New Testament scholar Ernst Käsemann (who himself experienced the apocalyptic struggle of the Confessing Church under Hitler)[2] forcefully argued that "apocalyptic is the mother of Christian theology."[3] He meant both that Jesus understood His messianic ministry, anointed in the Holy Spirit, as a battle against the unholy reign of Satan, and that the first Christians believed the word of His resurrection as God's apocalypse of His reign. Resurrection meant that in vindicating Jesus who had been crucified, God had exalted Him to God's "right hand"—not a spatial location but an omnipresent creative power—"until he has put all his enemies under his feet" (1 Cor. 15:25). Thus Luther retrieves and expresses the leading motif of New Testament apocalyptic theology in the first verse of "A Mighty Fortress": an overwhelming, devastating, and mysterious power of malice has usurped God's good earth and subjugated its life to the futility of injustice and death. God's faithful people groan under a cruel oppressor's rod. They live by faith, as Habakkuk prophesied, waiting for the promised victory of God.

To enter into the apocalyptic world of Luther and his Bible, modern people have to suspend disbelief about something. We have to allow Luther to figure this uncanny power of evil in the biblical character of Satan. We can bracket the question of the nature of Satan's reality for present purposes—that is a serious question of contemporary systematic theology. But for the purpose of studying Luther's claim to Christian truth, we have to deal with the *narrative* figure of the devil; the *Holy* Spirit makes no sense in the gospel *story* except as the person of God doing battle with the *unholy* spirits. This motif is indispensable to the gospel narrative, as Luther reads it.

In the figure of the "ancient foe," we are indeed confronted with the genuine radicalness of Luther's biblical theology with its challenge to "the easy conscience of modern man" (Reinhold Niebuhr) at home and at peace with massive and depersonalizing structures of malice. There is always a danger of superstition when we talk about "the devil." Luther himself, as we shall see, at times fell victim to it. But if we stay on our guard, we can by means of this figure of Satan enter into Luther's *radical* theology of the apocalyptic battle, which, like John the Baptist's axe, *cuts to the root* of our own cozy peace with malice taking malignant form in structures of injustice.

Samuel Beckett, in his 1950s existentialist tragicomedy *Waiting for Godot*, taunted his audience with the futility of endless waiting, a waiting that becomes habitual and results in sheer, senseless passivity. Luther, to an extent, shares the insight of the existentialists. We are captivated by overwhelming powers that dominate us and make us their puppets. Free will turns out to be but a pleasant illusion when all the choices we have are bad choices within a corrupt and captive world system from which there is no exit—until someone breaks in and sets us free from the strong man who masters the house (see Mark 3:27). We are not strong enough radically and consistently to stem the tide, but are swept away in its current. The very desires of our hearts are captured by the "bread and circuses"—that is, the living standards and entertainment spectacles of imperious powers. These powers own us. We become their puppets, or rather clowns, as in Beckett's play.

But Luther breaks with the existentialists because Someone has broken in for him and bound up that strong man. Existentialists, interestingly enough, are modern people who have inherited the apocalyptic worldview minus this inbreaking Liberator; they are like the ancient gnostics before them, who became disillusioned with the God of the Hebrew Scriptures after the Jewish revolts were crushed and lost faith in the living God promised them in the apocalyptic literature. Existentialists bravely draw the nihilistic conclusion of pure despair, that there is nothing to wait for even though the groaning life of a creation subjected to futility is just waiting for the world to change, as Romans 8 teaches. There is nothing to hope for. But Luther breaks with the existentialists because here and now, in this old aeon subjected to futility, a righteous man, a champion, a liberator chosen by God has appeared to win the battle for us all.

As a result, waiting in faith is transformed from futility to anticipation. Here and now, faith has something to see and receive, hence also to watch and to follow: Jesus Christ, who heals the sick, embraces the leper, feeds the hungry, expels the demons—all out of compassion for the people as for sheep without a shepherd! Here is our Victor! In naming the name of Jesus, Luther breaks with the existentialists trapped in the futility of endless waiting. They wait for something somehow better that never comes to a world where the more things change, the more they remain the same—eternally so! Their world, as Nietzsche captured in metaphysical poetry, is "the eternal return of the same." It is the eternal cosmic cycle anciently symbolized in the hooked cross (the Hakenkreuz or swastika), which the twentieth century's Nazis, in their nature worship, not accidentally appropriated. In such a world without transcendence, Luther finds in Jesus, who came once for all and still comes in the preaching of the gospel, a new ground of hope in the teeth of despair. As a result, a new kind of waiting becomes possible already now, the active waiting of faith receiving Jesus, operative in love. This hope is not optimism based on human calculation, but hope in God as our one, true, mighty fortress.

In hearing of Jesus Christ, those who believe are given a new personhood that becomes real and tangible, on the model of Paul's statement "It is no longer I who live, but it is Christ who lives in me. And the life I now live in the flesh I live by the faithfulness of the Son of God, who loved me and gave himself for me" (Gal. 2:20 NRSV altered). "Faith" is the name Luther gives to this new subjectivity, our incorporation into the faithfulness of Jesus Christ by the Holy Spirit rescuing us from unholy spirits.

Luther characteristically described this transformation of the existing self by the gospel word that comes from outside the self as the "joyful exchange." It is an exchange or circulation but not a quid pro quo, a calculating tit for tat. It is instead joyful because it gives precisely what is not deserved. It occurs whenever the gospel is rightly proclaimed such that Christ comes again to one by the Holy Spirit. Once and for all, Christ has entered into Satan's kingdom to make, amazingly enough, His own the sin of people by which Satan holds them captive—indeed, to give His own righteousness, Spirit, and life in place of sin and death.

Therefore believers can already now rise up, shake off their shackles, and follow the author and pioneer of their faith through many trials and tribulations on their freedom march. They are no longer owned by this sick and dying system of things but belong to God's coming reign. Here and now believers arise to new lives of *resistance*. "We tremble not for him; / his rage we can endure." These are words of resistance. Those who resist are the ones who have conquered fear and guilt because the desire of their very hearts has been captured by this champion who fights for them, Jesus Christ.

To understand Luther's theology here, we need to reflect on the nature of human desire. Luther has in mind Augustine's famous prayer from the beginning of his *Confessions*: "Thou hast made us for Thyself, and our hearts are restless until they find their rest in Thee, O God!" Human desire is polyvalent. It can go in any direction, be invested in any object. But it must go somewhere! We are natural creatures who seek the good and turn from evil. We must do this, since we do not have life in ourselves but must seek what is good from outside ourselves, as Luther explains the first article of the Apostles' Creed in his Large Catechism. Yet we restlessly chase goods that do not satisfy but rather at length addict us and finally degrade us, caught up as we are in Satan's shell game. Having lost God as the one true object of our heart's desire, at root we fear the pains and death of the body as the ultimate evil. As a result, we are tortured by the guilt of our failed souls that so easily agree to fatally compromised lives, unable to resist but rather finally obeisant to the tyrannical powers selling us false goods.

What changes us from pathetic and guilty minions of Satan into just and brave agents of the Holy Spirit is the coming of Jesus Christ into our midst. He captures the heart's desire not with silver and gold but with His own holy and precious blood, so that we may be His own, living under Him in His kingdom and serving Him in everlasting innocence and blessedness, as Luther explained the second article of the Creed in the Catechism. Jesus Christ, who comes to us and takes our place to bring us to God and one another, is the "one little word" from God that subdues the raging Satan and exorcizes the seductions by which he has gained human hearts. In the name of Jesus Christ, believers receive the power of resistance against the fear, guilt, and corruption all around us.

Some contemporary voices object to the military imagery of the Bible. They would certainly have to purge Luther's hymn from our singing as well! But this objection is based on a profound misunderstanding. It fears taking biblical metaphor literally. So naturally enough it wants to nip dangerous literalism in the bud by repudiating the military language for modeling violence and by looking to replace it with something else. It undertakes this revisionist surgery in place of the basic and essential pastoral work of interpreting biblical metaphor theologically as revealing God—which is what Luther does in the verses of "A Mighty Fortress Is Our God," the very title itself a mighty biblical *metaphor*.

To understand the difference between metaphor and literal interpretation, consider how metaphors have real reference in the world, even though this reference is to something new, perhaps surprising, and previously untold that must now be deciphered. Take an example: "Pastor Joe is a teddy bear." Literally, of course, this is nonsense. If I insisted that the statement's truth depends on its literal meaning, I would (unfortunately for Pastor Joe) have to dispatch him and send his corporal remains to a taxidermist for stuffing and stitching. So understood, we might then want to censure this dangerous imagery of pastors as teddy bears for inducing religious violence. Obviously, such an absurd procedure has missed the metaphor's very real function as reference altogether.

"Pastor Joe is a teddy bear" means that the consolation and comfort a child finds in such an ever-present companion *is* what people experience in Pastor Joe—a presence of comfort, encouragement, safety, and consolation. And that novel predication marks and reveals something real in the world, denoted by the metaphor when it is rightly interpreted and understood. Metaphors have such real reference by making novel predications through the rhetorical device of paradox. Paradox is not nonsense, unless we take it literally. Paradox employs the rhetoric of apparent contradiction in order to say and force recognition of something novel. In this way, paradox grabs attention to tell of things not yet known nor otherwise expressible.

The Letter to the Ephesians indicates this nonliteral but theologically real reference when it signals the right reading of the Bible's military metaphors: "Our struggle is not against enemies of blood and flesh, but against . . . the spiritual forces of evil in the heavenly places" (Eph. 6:12)—as in the figure of Satan, the "old evil foe." As conqueror of our fear and guilt, which make us liable to Satan, the Holy Spirit brings as His weapon not swords, tanks, cruise missiles, or predator drones but the new personhood in Christ endowed with the courage of faith, the power to resist in defiance of tyrants—the gifts of that very same Spirit who first led Jesus into battle against the unholy spirits when He arose from the baptismal waters of the river Jordan (Mark 1:12–13).

Let's sum up. In this overture we have been introduced to some of the leading motifs in Luther's theology. There is an overarching conflict between God and the devil, and we human beings are the prize. In this conflict we don't start from a neutral position but are born into a world in which our natural desire for God and one another in a beloved community has been captured by an uncanny destroyer making us his guilty and fear-ridden puppets or clowns. Yet a champion, Jesus Christ, has appeared in the very midst of this captivity and burst its bonds to set us free from both the guilt and the power of sin. He has done so by taking on Himself our sin and death to give us in their place His life and righteousness. Now awash with His own Spirit, we take the stand as courageous witnesses to the reign of

God, our one and true mighty fortress. Thus fortified, we get to live new lives of faithful resistance already now—no longer conformed to this world but transformed (Rom. 12:2)—until that mighty fortress of righteousness, life, and peace comes visibly in all power and glory.

> Let goods and kindred go,
> this mortal life also;
> the body they may kill:
> God's truth abideth still;
> his kingdom is forever!

The key word: *resistance*!

PART 1

Luther in Evangelical Perspective

1

The New Birth

LUTHER'S HYMN "To Jordan Came the Christ Our Lord"[1] comes from late in Luther's life (1541). For him, the baptism of Jesus marks the epiphany or manifestation of the mystery of the Holy Trinity. The Voice from heaven attests Jesus's Sonship and seals this attestation with the anointing of the Spirit in the figure of the dove. In Luther's hymn it is just this coordination of baptism and the Trinity of Father, Son, and Holy Spirit that is taken up from the patristic tradition. Indeed, what is striking is Luther's grounding of the baptismal death of the sinner and resurrection of the believer in the narrative theology of trinitarian advent.

The word spoken by God the Father to Jesus the beloved Son and sealed with the anointing of the Spirit in the figure of the dove in verses 3–4 of Luther's hymn becomes the same word spoken to every Christian in baptism in verse 5, as if to say, "You too are my beloved son/daughter united by the Spirit with your brother, Jesus Christ, in his death and resurrection" (see appendix). This mediation of Christ's filial relation to God as Father to the believer is possible because, as his verse 5 shows, Luther's narrative interpretation of the baptism story, in tandem with the transfiguration story, anticipates the Easter vindication of the Crucified One.

Jesus is not refuted! He is not defeated! He is risen! After death at cross and tomb, He proves indeed to be God's gracious Word of mercy to all humanity. Therefore, listen to Him! It is the Father who reveals the man Jesus as the beloved Son and thus directs our attention to Him by the sending of the Spirit—an *epistemic principle* to which Luther returns in the final verse when he contrasts the perspective of unbelieving reason to the new eyes given in faith.

Luther thus holds to what might be called "perspectivalism." Luther is not a commonsense realist. Nor is he an idealist. But, just as vision is determined by perspective, the knowledge of God is determined by the perspectives of belief and disbelief at the announcement (*kerygma*) in the name of God: "You too are my beloved son/ daughter united by the Spirit with your brother, Jesus Christ, in his death and resurrection."

All critical thinking distinguishes between reality and appearance. But in our Western tradition we have predominantly done this in Plato's way: behind the flux of sense experience there is a true, intellectual, unchanging formal reality that is the true object of purified, intellectual knowledge. Luther breaks with this Platonism. For him, all down-to-earth perspectives are true insofar as they see what they see. Apart from lying, the angle of vision truly captures anyone's particular take on things from their finite perspective. However, human beings are tempted to claim more for their snapshots of reality than these snapshots can or do represent, as if they were universal or scientific or represented expert knowledge of the whole. But a perspective of the whole is possible only from God's omniscient perspective, not a creature's. In fact, all human perspectives are finite and partial. Only God knows the whole. That is how Luther distinguishes the knowledge of the creature from that of the Creator.

Thus human beings in the light of nature truly see the crucified man—rejected, betrayed, abandoned by all—and say, "This is the end, this is the whole sum of the matter." But that conclusion is only part of the story. It is not the whole of the matter. If faith sees in this same crucified man the Lamb of God who takes away the sin of the world, it sees Jesus in what can only be God's own perspective, as the beloved Son of the Father's own eternal and boundless compassion, the prolepsis (revelation in advance) of the end of history (the last judgment, the denouement, the revelation of the whole).

That Christian faith, according to Luther, sees and thus also knows things in a new and divine perspective is something astonishing. This knowledge comes not by nature from human power but by the light of grace that shines in the darkness of the light of nature. In verses 5–7 of the hymn, Luther spells out the new subjectivity of believers bequeathed by baptismal union with Christ. To paraphrase: "You too are beloved children, unconditionally objects of God's eternal favor. As such, you too are anointed with the Spirit to rise up as new subjects in lifelong battle *against* the unholy powers and battle *for* the healing of the nations." So believers see *the world*, beginning with their own *selves*, in the new perspective of reconciliation in Christ: sinful but passionately loved, damaged but being healed, hopelessly ruined so far as human power can repair but still to be redeemed by the One to whom all things are possible. Such new vision is not a spectator sport to be contemplated at leisure. It grips believers with the divine passion, which does not leave them dead in their sins but spurs them on to new lives of resistance.

A corresponding warning is issued in verse 6 of Luther's hymn. It is a warning against despising this grace, which has given new birth, and persisting with Adam's old subjectivity: "His holiness avails him not, / Nor aught which he is doing." Ever surprisingly with Luther, it is the "religious" person, the one who persists in striving and working to merit grace, who is revealed as the enemy of divine gifts freely given. The reason for this surprising judgment is that religion remains within the perspective of the light of nature; it is the sincere and thinking person's natural desire to avoid punishment and earn a reward transferred from worldly relations to the relationship with God. This act of transference is the root of idolatry for Luther, not images as such. For under the guise of piety, religion really worships its own works or devotions and robs the true God of the glory of grace. The gift of grace freely given is not an idea or a doctrine. It is not a principle or an insight. It is not even a correct image or idea of God. The gift freely given is the new humanity—namely, the Person at the center of trinitarian advent, Jesus Christ—and consequently Holy Spirit union with Him in the new subjectivity Luther calls faith.

As Dietrich Bonhoeffer, a latter-day theologian who knew Luther well, taught, Jesus Christ is "the Man for others." It is His work, expressing His person as the Father's beloved Son, that is truly good and truly gift. Thus one can participate in this good work of Christ alone first of all *only* as a recipient of it, dying with Christ to sinful self-seeking and religious self-assertion in order to arise in His Spirit to new life for others. This reception of union with Christ is what baptism is and effects, where and when it pleases God.

Unfortunately, ever since the Reformation the issue of baptism has revolved around the extremes of sacramental rebirth on account of the infusion of infant faith, on the one side, and the believer's baptism as her outward testimony to an inner conversion experience, on the other. In historical truth, Luther was provoked at the emergence of the latter stance by the offensive practice of rebaptizing adults. This offended Luther because rebaptism cannot but imply the illegitimacy of the baptizing church and the invalidity of its ministry. It is difficult for those practicing believer's baptism to see this offense, since for them baptism is the believer's act, and one might feel free to be rebaptized as often as one feels the need! What clears up this dispute is the contention that baptism is a sign for union with the tomb of Christ, His once-and-for-all death, which is effective where and when it pleases the Spirit to unify the sign with the thing signified, the crucified and risen Lord Jesus.

Luther affirmed the possibility of the infusion of infant faith because for him faith is essentially trusting reception, not an adult decision. What more is a baby, he reasoned, than trusting reception of the loving care offered to it? Even more importantly, however, Luther affirmed infant baptism because he wanted to preserve the gift character of baptism, even though this led him to affirm things that in truth became the basis for vast abuse in so-called *Kulturprotestantismus* ("acculturated Protestantism"; see further below).

Most "mainline" Protestants in North America hold some awkward combination of the two views: we baptize infants as heirs of the parents' faith, or we regard baptism as an act of dedicating the infant to God or as a rite of passage "welcoming" babies into the world. These rationalizations have little to do with dying and rising in union with Christ! All these incoherent compromises progressively strip baptism of the christological and trinitarian content that Luther's hymn so robustly lifts up.

We ought to see that all of these latter compromises lend truth to the observations made by critics that historical Lutheranism with its cheap-grace, blank-check practice of baptizing children, no questions asked, has lost Luther's prophetic edge and become a religious sacralization of "this world," not transformative but conformist. Exasperation with this, especially after the failure to reckon deeply with the sins of the Lutheran church in Germany during the Nazi era, led Karl Barth late in life to reject infant baptism as the root of compromised Christianity in the modern period.[2] Certainly, believer's baptism is no less prone to such abuse. In evangelical and free churches, "conversion" has become as routinized and conformist as infant baptism, producing, as it did, "born again" slaveholders and Jim Crow segregationists just like baptized Nazis. In *either* case, we are missing something important to which Luther points in connecting baptism with the advent of the Holy Trinity.

Let me put it this way: it does not matter psychologically or biographically whether one comes to faith before or after the sign, which is water baptism, is administered, because whatever way (psychologically speaking) we come to faith in the Christian sense, it is always by the Spirit's speaking the gospel and giving us ears to truly hear. It is always oriented, whether biographically forward or backward, to the very same Word that is dramatically and publicly enacted in baptism: namely, that Jesus with His cross gives us Himself as a gift—that is, gives His own filial relation to God to those who surrender their sinfulness to Him. To force a choice between infant and believer's baptism turns attention away from this one Word of God that we are to hear, trust, and obey in life and in death. It leads us down a blind alley, seeking some supposedly normative order of religious or psychological experience. But one can enter the Christian faith, psychologically speaking, in about as many ways as there are persons. In every case, it is the Christian faith that goes public as baptism into union with Christ in His death and resurrection.

What really matters, in other words, is not psychology but theology: that the faith to which one is born anew is the faith of the *Holy* Spirit, cleaving to the *Son*, directed to the *Father's* reign and glory. This matters because it is the faithfulness of Jesus Christ, to us sinners as to His Father, that now echoes in our weak faith, created by the same Spirit who led faithful Jesus through the cross to the crown, for us and for all. Just as people come to Christian faith in all sorts of ways, the gospel word of God is communicated in an infinite variety of ways: not only in the sermon on Sunday or the meal of the baptized, but also in reading, in conversation, by experiences of Christian community or vivid examples of sanctified living, and so on.

If this coming to faith is what really matters, it means—in our post-Christendom situation—getting used to adult conversion and thus the need to offer lifelong Christian learning in serious catechesis, as in the ancient church or in today's Roman Catholic Rite of Christian Initiation for Adults. Unfortunately, one fears, many American Christians are so desperate for dues-paying members that, under the guise of "inclusiveness" or "soul-saving," we "take 'em in, no questions asked," claiming a market niche in grace so cheap you can't give it away. But in his hymn, Luther puts together what we have torn apart:

> Thus Jesus His disciples sent
> Go, teach ye every nation,
> That, lost in sin, they must repent,
> And flee from condemnation.

An inclusive gospel invitation and a fiery repentance that melts us individually and remolds us into Christ's body in the world belong together when the theological point of baptism is inclusion in the holy life of the Trinity.

Faith in Christ

But this inclusion is by faith and not by sight! It comes from God—who comes to us by His word! The baptism of Jesus was the breakthrough of the promised future of eternal life with God into our present. Our baptism into Christ is just the same as the Spirit's breakthrough into this present evil age. As a result, for Luther, Spirit-given faith alone justifies, yet faith alone also works. There is a "patiency" in Christ—a suffering of divine things—that births a new agency in Christ. In the treatise *Two Kinds of Righteousness* (1519),[3] the young Luther accordingly explores the proper distinction between Christ's righteousness given to us as a gift by Spirit-given faith (patiency) and our own proper righteousness (agency). In the power of this gift of Christ by the Spirit, the newborn believer co-operates with God to do the same good works of Christ in love and mercy.

Luther's Latin word *alienus* (alien) for this righteousness of Christ given to the believer as a gift is likely to alienate us today! That is to say, to us this word means something "out of this world," as in an alien spaceship, something strange or exotic or foreign. But we have to put these connotations aside to understand Luther's meaning when he argues in this short treatise that the Christian's righteousness is, first and foremost, "alien." By this he simply means that the Christian's righteousness is first—and ever first—the deed and hence the property of Jesus Christ. In the Latin of Luther's day, the opposite of the word "alien" is "proper" (Latin *proprium*)—that is, something that is properly my own, my own "property," because I am the doer of the deed or the one who acquired the "property" by my own sweat and toil.

By this antonym we see that what is "alien" is simply the property of someone other than myself, because this other person has acquired it by her own doing. Christ's righteousness, then, is His own property, acquired by His own loving obedience in His life's deed of love, culminating in His death on the cross in solidarity with the sinners whose sins He has forgiven, whose diseases He has borne, whose death He now makes His own. This solidarity of love with sinners all the way down to dying their death is the "property" of Jesus that God the Father recognizes and vindicates on Easter morn, indeed declaring it to be His very own righteousness of mercy and love. It is not a righteousness, then, that Christ possesses quiescently—that is, as a passive quality of nature—but rather a righteousness uniquely acquired in history by faithful obedience to death, even death on a cross. This righteousness is, then, Christ Himself in His finished work on the cross, taken as the unique biographical event of the incarnate Son, or—in Paul's words from Galatians 2:20 that Luther loves—of "the Son of God, who loved me and gave himself for me."

He *gave*. This righteousness is the *gift* of Himself for others, a self-*donation*. He intends it to become "ours." As with any true gift, the giver hands over possession so that the property, as Luther insists, truly becomes "ours," just as if we had been the proper doers of it. As Christ in His righteousness has made us who are sinners His own, so we who are sinners make this Christ-for-us our own life and righteousness by faith, which trustingly receives the loving care. Faith is thus the personal "taking hold" of the gift, the "letting it be" of those gifted, the appropriation "for me," so that His righteousness truly becomes our own, just as Christ the Giver intends.

Yet this "having" of faith is as "having not" (see 1 Cor. 7:29–31), since Christ in His righteousness does not cease to be Christ the Giver, just as a spouse in a marriage does not cease to be a historical human individual. Christ's righteousness, then, *dwells* in us by faith, as Luther thinks of the other part of Galatians 2:20, "Christ who lives in me." Moreover, it is the risen, living Jesus Christ in and as His righteousness that, living in me, grows daily, increasing His sway and establishing His dominion—"baking," as Luther says elsewhere, Christ and the believer "into one loaf." Since the righteousness of Christ was His loving obedience *for us*, as indwelling gift it works this same loving obedience of faith *in us*—just as spouses in a good marriage grow together as one. Yet, since this marriage of Christ and faith is not between equals, it is always in that specific order according to which the alien righteousness of what Christ did *for us* apart from us and before us precedes the effective gift of this loving obedience *in us,* so that the alien righteousness of Christ is and remains the "basis and source of our own actual righteousness."

So our own proper righteousness is likened to that of the spouse who replies to the promise of the beloved, "I am yours," with "Amen, and you are mine." Secured in this nuptial new covenant of love, the believer is liberated by it for a new life of service in the needy world, no longer seeking a righteousness of one's own with which to secure life, but rather righteously seeking "only the welfare of others." This liberated or freed seeking of the good of others norms and guides the Christian's own "proper" righteousness; that is to say, it specifies which works are truly good.

It may help here to understand the ambiguity of the term "good works," which was batted around in Reformation-era controversies. In Luther's time, "good works" had come to refer to the "religious" works of serious individuals concerned to secure eternal salvation for themselves, such as pilgrimages, fasts, flagellations, attendance at Mass, monastic vows, and so on. By such religious works, called "good," believers sought to secure for themselves the property of righteousness before God as the sincere doers of serious deeds of personal sacrifice that would merit eternal recognition. In this sense of "religious" works, Luther attacks the "good works" of his day to deny that they can do for us what only Christ does for sinners— namely, make us righteous by His own living, dying, and reigning eternally for us.

In contrast to religious works and other pious devotions motivated by avoiding the pains of hell and gaining the reward of heaven, Christ's righteousness, acquired by His own unique loving obedience to death, even death on the cross, is the one truly "good work." He is the new and true Adam, the model of God for true humanity. He in person is the basis of any good works Christians do, because by the forgiveness of sins He liberates them from the hopeless and, at root, self-centered effort to merit forgiveness and secure salvation, and in so doing becomes the norm that judges and decides what is truly "good" about a work. As Paul says in Philippians 2:5: "Let the same mind be in you that was in Christ Jesus."

Faith in Society

From these reflections, we can see today the world-historical revolution that Luther launched with this line of thought: he made secular life holy, or better, capable of sanctification—"washing the baby's diapers to the glory of God," as he once described a Christian man's new work in God's world (with characteristic flair against the gender stereotypes of the time). As Christ came into the world, into Galilee, and at last into the tomb, so true holiness is acquired not by flight from the world into self-chosen religious works but, as the commandments of God specify, in the worldly stations of marriage and family life, on the job and in school, in the law court and in the court of public opinion, in the marketplace and on the police force. Life in the world becomes the arena of "sanctification," the place for the performance of the Christian's own proper righteousness—truly good, truly righteous work, because it seeks not its own welfare but that of others. As a result, "you are powerful, not that you may make the weak weaker by oppression, but that you may make them powerful by raising them up and defending them." Five hundred years later, we are still coming to terms with Luther's insight here!

The reason we are still working out Luther's insight in this connection is that it is one thing to understand that sin is robbery that takes the glory of our salvation away from God by robbing the neighbor in need of our love. That is but the flip side of affirming that faith gives God all the glory for His rich mercy in Christ by giving all our love to the neighbor in need. Understanding this is one thing. It is quite another thing to live this way. In this latter sense, Luther thinks that a true Christian is a "rare bird" and that it is accordingly not possible, nor does God desire, to govern civic life with the gospel of Christ's righteousness in the same way that the gospel ought to govern the life of the church—as if we could legally institute Christian marriage or a Christian law court or a Christian marketplace or a Christian police force, and so on. Christianity for Luther is not a jurisprudence (he burned the books of canon law along with the papal bull), as in rabbinic Judaism or Islamic sharia, but rather an ethic of faith active in love. But is the unintended consequence of this reformation of morals, as Brad Gregory argues, the catalyst for contemporary secularism?[4]

Yes and no. The delimitation of the civic realm to affairs of this life—notably by denying the state's competence to judge matters of conscience or questions of theology—certainly is a long-term result of Luther's reformation. But the ideology of autonomous reason and its capacity to rule also over matters of conscience—Kant's Tribunal of Reason—cannot be so understood. Luther holds that the law of Moses, which is also the "natural" law written on human hearts, must reign in the tense interim time between the ascension of Christ and His return in glory. The natural law is nothing other than the rules that natural human reason discerns for living together socially in peace and equity in the civic institutions of marriage and marketplace, the law court, and even so-called organized religion.

The gospel brings clarity to this natural law obscured by sin, because it knows the loving intention of the divine lawgiver, revealed in Christ, who stands behind the natural law. It knows this divine intention from Moses as further clarified by Christ, especially in His preaching of the heavenly Father in the Sermon on the Mount. But Christian insight into God's purpose, summed up in the double love commandment, does not supplant civic law with a revealed legislation that coerces faith and conscience. Rather, natural law coerces the disobedient, who know in their conscience the difference between right and wrong but are unwilling to abide by it. There are several reasons for this.

Primary for Luther is that faith, which must be voluntary if it is to be true, is betrayed if it is forced by the legal power of the state. Coercion makes only hypocrites, not Christians. The state, moreover, is not competent to judge questions of faith, which is a task Luther assigns to theologians, pastors, and also the baptized people of God, who hear the voice of the shepherd and will not listen to a stranger (see John 10:5, 27). Because of sin, however, the state is always a coercive order that compels the disobedient; otherwise it fails to protect the obedient. Qualitatively different from the servile and coerced obedience under the law, gospel and faith must be freely given and freely received by newborn believers adopted into a filial relation to God and thus a loving and willing obedience. Life in civil society, therefore, is mixed. In the social life together of the obedient and disobedient, many lesser evils must be tolerated if the even greater evil of a tyranny of the righteous majority coercing theological correctness is to be avoided. After 1521, Luther lived his life as a condemned heretic. He knew firsthand the evil that comes from the confusion of the regimes of law and of gospel by which God governs the fraught world in the interim between Christ's ascension and parousia.

In Christian life, even socially tolerated evils are to be known and confessed as sinful before God. This acknowledgment of sinfulness in civil righteousness serves as a check against zealotry by reminding the Christian conscience of the moral ambiguities involved in public vocations, which work in degrees of greater and lesser good or evil, not in apocalyptic, hence categorical, oppositions. An example of this today might be state-run gambling, as in lotteries, to fund public education. This is an idolatry, worshiping the goddess Fortuna, known in colloquial English as "Lady Luck." It institutes an injustice, exploiting the poor who can hardly afford to waste precious dollars on one-in-a-million chances at making a million, while neglecting a proportionate taxation of those better off to fund quality education for all. Yet if the state did not so monopolize the vice of gambling, organized crime would be back in town running the "numbers" racket.

Luther writes, "It is [the state's] necessary function to punish and judge evil men, to vindicate and defend the oppressed, because it is not [the state], but God who does this," drawing on Paul's teaching in Romans 13. Often overlooked in this connection, however, is the statement in Romans 13:5 that Christians render political obedience on account of "conscience," which means responsibility to God for that portion of creation entrusted to one's care as a person made in His image for attaining His likeness. Conscientious responsibility to God thus entails conscientious objection when the state does not judge evil or defend the oppressed.

Luther could not have defied emperor as well as pope on the grounds of a conscience captive to the Word of God if this reading of holy secularity did not subordinate political obedience to God's higher authority and law of holy love. The lawful state is commissioned to do God's strange work of love, constraining what is against love. In this sense, Luther boasts that he is the first theologian in a thousand years to lift up and exalt the "holy secularity" of civil government. We have here the first inklings of Luther's difficult but crucial "doctrine of the two kingdoms": this is simply the transposition of his teaching about the two kinds of righteousness, or about the proper distinction of God's Word as law and as gospel, into the sphere of social ethics.

Faith as a Gift

In his *Preface to Romans*[5] (1522, reworked in 1546), Luther articulated Paul's theme of faith as the gift of the Holy Spirit, faith that receives and begins to live the gift that is Jesus Christ, our righteousness. Luther's controversial doctrine at the time was not justification by grace. He and his better opponents agreed that justification was by grace, indeed, by grace alone—a Catholic stance later endorsed by the Council of Trent. They differed in that for Luther the justifying grace of Christ becomes effective personally, *pro me* (for me), by the Spirit's grace in bestowing *faith*. Faith comes to me and overtakes me, the sinner, who otherwise does not and cannot believe in the man crucified in my place, hence cannot personally surrender to the merciful Christ who, risen and vindicated, is truly there "for me." This gift of the Spirit enabling surrender to the loving claim of the crucified and risen Christ, "I am yours and you are mine," is the new birth. Spirit-given faith *is* the new birth.

That teaching could and did sound like the infused grace of medieval theology, based on Augustine's favorite Bible verse in Romans about the love of God poured into our hearts by the Holy Spirit, who is given to us (Rom. 5:5). This appearance of infused grace would cause controversy later and force the abstract clarification that righteousness is first imputed and only as such also infused. The necessity of the later clarification was to preclude introspection into the state of one's soul or emotions and rather direct the doubting soul in its trials to "extraspection," so to speak, staying focused on Christ, who comes to the self from outside the self to transform the self.

But in 1522 Luther's controversial teaching, to be precise, was that such personally appropriating faith justifies—faith in Christ, to be sure, but all the same *faith*, faith *alone* in Christ alone. Such faith, defined as a gift of the Spirit, is not and cannot be a human work, a mere opinion about Christ, even about Christ alone as Savior of the world. It is the trust *ex corde*, "from the heart," created by the Spirit who reveals the dying Jesus as the Lamb of God who takes away the sin of the world, hence also *pro me*, taking away *my* sin too so that I, personally, am slain spiritually by this news and reconstituted utterly in my subjectivity. In the *Preface to Romans*, Luther accentuates this doctrine of Spirit-rendered personal faith, the gift to receive the gift that is Jesus Christ. Famously, it was this text, *Preface to Romans*, read aloud in the hearing of John Wesley (the founder of Methodism) a century and a half later, that caused Wesley's *heart* to feel "strangely warmed"—the beginning of his personal conversion, just as Luther had intended in composing those words.

In the previous discussion, we observed how Luther sharply distinguished between the outward or external *observance* of the commandments that produces civic righteousness, the kind of justice that lawyers and philosophers understand, and the righteousness of the inner person that *fulfills* the commandments by doing all things in trust toward God and in love for others. The difference for Luther is that under the system of law, my good behavior, or avoidance of bad behavior, is always motivated by enlightened self-interest before the court of public opinion. So no matter how enlightened I am and how good my behavior is for others, the agent at work here is still the old, self-seeking self, seeking a reward or avoiding a penalty.

For Luther, divine law does *not* mean the Ten Commandments as opposed to, for example, the Criminal Code of Virginia. For God the Creator to be a Judge means something other than adjudicating justice through the Commandments or the Criminal Code. Divine law is the Creator coming as Judge of the creature; as the prophets teach, God searches and judges the heart. And here, what the Judge is looking for is the creature's "willing pleasure" in God's will.[6]

Note well: taking pleasure in God's will—that is, loving God's will from the biblical seat of the person, "the heart," emotions and all— does not mean merely observing the law, but fulfilling it. This "willing pleasure" produces the spontaneous doing of good that pleases God and fulfills the commandments. Such "willing pleasure" in God's will cannot be acquired by natural powers alone; fallen humanity has a corrupted nature, without faith and without the Spirit, that takes will- ing pleasure in wanting to be God and not wanting God to be God. Willing pleasure in God's will, however, is filial, like that of loving children toward loving parents, not servile, like that of slaves toward harsh masters. To acquire such filial, willing pleasure in God's will, the fallen creature must be born anew, must be granted the power to become a child of God. Believers are born anew when their affective apparatus is transformed by the Spirit, who sheds the love of God abroad in their hearts, so that they in willing pleasure cry, in union with the Son, "Abba! Father!"

Thus, traditional criticism (*both* Catholic *and* Protestant) of the doctrine of justification by faith is misplaced if it argues that, for Luther, Christ's righteousness remains alien and external, never touching and transforming the heart. This criticism may well apply to the version of the doctrine of justification that prevailed in later Lutheranism, which, along the lines indicated above, separated out the imputation, or accreditation, of Christ's righteousness to the sinner and referred to this abstracted imputation ("forensic" imputa- tion, like the pronouncement of acquittal by a judge) as justification, strictly speaking. Here forensic or imputative justification is separated in principle from sanctification, or becoming righteous, which fol- lows (maybe, fingers crossed, hopefully) as the human response to imputed righteousness. But notice, upon reading Luther's account in the *Preface to Romans*, how this later Lutheran doctrine cannot be squared with Luther's own teaching.

As faith is a divine *work and gift of the Spirit*, and as sin is any- thing done in unfaith, justifying faith is already regeneration or sanctification. In this light, we can even suggest that Wesley was right—in the name of the Luther of the *Preface to Romans*—to criticize orthodox Lutheranism's strictly extrinsic or forensic explanation of justification. One cannot separate Christ for us from Christ in us, since we cannot have either without the Spirit persuading us that Christ is for us, sinners. And this persuasion to trust in Christ *is* Christ at work in us—just as the joyful exchange depicts.

Luther's teaching that faith regenerates differs in this way from the teachings of Andreas Osiander, the early follower of Luther who taught infused righteousness, against whom early Lutheranism overreacted. Osiander erroneously took Luther's faith that fulfills the law *ex corde* as the supernatural effect of the quality of divine righteousness being infused into the soul, like water being poured into an empty vessel. Thus he pictured grace effecting the new birth magically, as a supernatural power that transforms us impersonally, apart from the personal encounter with Christ in repentance and faith on the historical occasion of preaching the external word of the gospel, which tells of Christ's obedience for us to death, even death on a cross. An indication of how Luther differs from Osiander may be seen in Luther's stress on the special work of faith as the *mortification of the flesh*—necessary if faith is obedience to the gospel and its righteousness is our personal conformation to Christ's death and resurrection. But the task of mortification of the flesh is hardly necessary if one is healed, as it were, by swallowing a divine potion!

The mature Luther refined his teaching on justification to guard against Osiander's misunderstanding of it, but he never retracted the view that "faith, that work of the Spirit," justifies and is therefore already *regeneration* and thus the beginning of *sanctification*. There is an abstract, logical priority of imputation over regeneration: Christ for us is the basis of Christ in us. But Christ is not divided into a base package with added options. If one must employ an abstraction to attain clarity about this, one can rightly say that God imputes or accredits the righteousness of Christ to the believer, whom God therewith renews on that basis. So even the holiest Christian, to whom grace is not given in vain, who loves God above all and all creatures in and under God, nonetheless sings, "Nothing in my hands I bring, solely to thy cross I cling."

Indeed, it is just this believer who takes "willing pleasure" in God's will to save by utter grace. One believes this, or one has no true faith that justifies at all. Grace makes the commandments of God "dear" to the heart, or one has no true faith that justifies at all. Grace gives true freedom "from sin, . . . a freedom only to do good with pleasure and to live without the compulsion of the law," or one has no true faith that justifies at all. "Our freedom is, therefore, no carefree fleshly freedom which is not obligated to do anything, but a freedom that does many works of all kinds." Christian freedom is the freedom to love.

The *Preface to Romans* concludes with a brief but powerful meditation on predestination, since Paul takes up this topic in Romans 9–11. Luther makes the simple but powerful point that the doctrine of predestination takes salvation out of the creature's hands and puts it into God's, freeing those chosen and called from religious self-concern. Luther does not, on the whole, think of election as having taken place in the eternal past of God's absolute decree; rather, as we have seen, since faith is the Spirit's work and gift through the preaching of the gospel, Luther sees election occurring where and when the Spirit pleases, in the giving of the gift of justifying faith. On this mysterious topic, however, perspective matters.

Luther admonishes us to approach the doctrine of predestination after the model of Paul in Romans, as a doxological reflection coming at the end of our examination of the gospel's revelation of the saving righteousness of God in Christ. Then it becomes clear that Jesus Christ is not God's second thought, as if, surprised, God had thought, "Adam sinned. Oh no, now what do I do?" Rather, from all eternity Adam's redemption in Christ has been God's *first* thought, *first* in the very creation of the world, hence God's self-predestination, so to speak, to love us in the beloved Son. In this case, predestination would be something more like God's free self-determination to be the God of grace for us (as Karl Barth taught centuries later). "For God has imprisoned all in disobedience so that he may be merciful

to all"—so Paul concludes in Romans 11:32. And it is just this culminating thought (*not* then the thought of God's inscrutable decree
fating some to reprobation but others to salvation) that causes Paul
to burst into praise at the depth and wisdom of God's ways. But if
we inquire into predestination apart from following the way of Paul
in Romans, and instead speculate about how to reconcile the sovereignty of God with human freedom, we enter into a labyrinth from
which there is no exit but only a dizzying vertigo.

The Development of Luther's Doctrine of Justification

In his "Preface to the Complete Edition of Luther's Latin Writings"
(1545),[7] the aged Luther recalls his struggle to understand Paul's claim
that the righteousness of God is revealed in the gospel and his discovery of the righteousness by which God makes the ungodly righteous
through the gift of faith in Jesus Christ. Predictably, "lucubration"
is not a word one will have yet encountered in life. Not until, that
is, reading the first lines of a rarely chagrined Luther in this preface
to the publication of his Latin writings in 1545 (the year before his
death), where he makes an open admission of the "unsystematic"
nature of his writings.

The Latin word *lucubratio* refers to "burning the midnight oil"—
that is, reading and writing by candlelight or oil lamp; the sense then
is "nocturnal studies." So the old man Luther refers to the treatises
composed in Latin and now collected for republication after some
twenty-five years of theological controversy. Luther contrasts the
"chaos" of his "nocturnal studies" with the "systematic" writings
of his colleague, Melanchthon, whose calm and deliberate studies are
pedagogically well organized for ease of reader understanding. He
apologizes for the relative disorder of his own writings, due to their
ad hoc composition; they were written, he explains, under pressure
to respond to the urgent demands of the hour. Luther often had to
bone up on the issues by late-night study, and then, without the aid
of word processing (let us contemporaries note!), draft and redraft by
hand until he could no longer delay publishing something that spoke

to the latest emergency. So chaotic are his writings, he acknowledges, that even he has trouble making sense of them!

Certainly Luther's penchant for rhetorical excess and his personally volatile nature contribute to the impression of chaos. But this honest acknowledgment of the state of emergency in which Luther composed should not mislead us into thinking that his theology is not "systematic" in the sense of being internally consistent and forming a coherent whole—even if it leaves us with the task of sorting some things out. Luther was a principled thinker; he was anything but an opportunist—the political hack, cozying up to the princes as enemies depicted him. There is, to be sure, genuine development in his thought. Indeed, Luther takes care to describe that development to the readers of this preface; but development should not be regarded as a mark of inconsistency.

For example, if we look at Luther's theology with respect to the doctrine of God, Luther is consistently and emphatically trinitarian from beginning to end; if we look at his Christology, Luther consistently and emphatically teaches the Christ of the "joyful exchange" from even before the time of his Reformation "breakthrough." When we look at his theological anthropology, from beginning to end Luther follows Augustine in thinking of human beings as true creatures, whose seat of desire in the heart is objectively determined by the need for God above all and for one another in beloved community, even if subjectively they can find neither in their lost and corrupted state. But as we noted above, because of the Osiander controversy Luther was forced to refine his doctrine of justification to the end of his life. Thus when we turn to his famous teaching on how the sinner becomes righteous before God, we can trace some—subtle—development. Luther himself calls it to our attention in this preface.

In his earliest theology we see Luther following Augustine, teaching that the sinner becomes righteous before God by the humility of repentance and faith—in other words, whoever humbly confesses sin tells the truth and justifies God in His judgment and just so becomes righteous before God. To humbly confess sins, however, exceeds the sinner's power. Only the hardened heart melted by the infusion of soul-transforming grace can tell the truth about itself. The humbled sinner then is justified by this grace, "because God's love has been poured into our hearts through the Holy Spirit" (Rom. 5:5). Without ever rejecting this theme from Augustine, the early Luther teaches further, as we saw in the *Preface to Romans*, how by the Spirit's grant of faith, as the gift to receive the gift of Christ, the sinner is justified not merely by grace—there was no dispute about that—but precisely by the Spirit-given faith that takes hold of the justice of Christ and makes it one's own.

What has intervened, as we saw, is the Osiander controversy. Osiander took the infusion of grace not as the message of the personal and historical righteousness of Christ, who loved me and gave himself for me, but rather as a natural divine property of holiness supernaturally infused into the soul. This misunderstanding threatened once again to restore religious self-preoccupation. Rather than faith looking to Christ as its righteousness, now anxious believers would have to look at the state of their own souls to detect transformation. So, in this late work, as Luther recapitulates autobiographically the development of his doctrine of justification, we see how he defines the event of justification more strictly as an imputation from outside the self—that is, as the accrediting of Christ's obedience to the disobedient sinner who nevertheless believes, resulting in the nonreckoning of the believing sinner's remaining sin. Abstractly speaking, then, imputation is not to be confused with regeneration, the new birth of the soul, even if concretely the two go together and are inseparable. That is in fact, Luther now believes, a fresh and more precise way of expressing the matter. For us to appreciate it, however, we have to appreciate what "abstractions" are good for.

Luther argues that, taken abstractly, justification as such (that is, as separated in thought from regeneration and/or sanctification) is the imputation of Christ's alien righteousness by which sins are forgiven and the sinner is deemed righteous in God's eyes. This picture is an abstraction; that is to say, it abstracts from the personal faith that receives, permits, and takes hold of Christ's righteousness because the Holy Spirit has opened heart and mind to receive Him.

This abstraction is performed for the sake of conceptual clarity. The value of this abstraction is to show that, no matter how far in the Christian life a believer progresses, she will never rely on her progress but even in the course of very real progress will rely on God's imputation for Christ's sake: "Nothing in my hands I bring, simply to thy cross I cling." Yet an abstraction (*fides abstracta*, as Luther actually calls it) is abstracted from the real, biographical faith of a believer in a body here on the earth, receiving, permitting, and taking hold. Here Luther speaks of *fides incarnata*, an "incarnate faith," which is concretely always a Christ-formed faith regenerating the person and becoming operative in love.

Thus, even at this late date and in spite of the development in the doctrine of justification to a more correct and precise abstraction regarding imputation, Luther is still expressly crediting Augustine's writing *On the Spirit and the Letter* as the model and inspiration for his own development of the doctrine of justification. For here he learned that the gift of faith to receive the gift of Christ is also the gracious work of God the Holy Spirit.

This preface is also interesting for the history it gives of the outbreak of the controversy from a local dispute about the selling of indulgences into a full-scale confrontation over the authority of the pope. Luther assigns the indulgence controversy both to the "greed" of the regional warrior-bishops of those days (before the reforms of the Council of Trent), who raked in a percentage from the sale of the indulgences, and to the ambition of his opponent, Johannes Eck, who ingratiated himself to Rome as more papist than the popes themselves.

There is an interesting difference in perspectives here that in some degree abides to this day. From the Protestant perspective, the Reformation was a tragic *necessity*, because the sale of indulgences, backed up by the false authority claimed for the papacy, obscured the pure gift of the gospel—and that is an intolerable offense that gives legitimate cause for division. From the Catholic perspective, the Reformation was a *tragic* necessity, because the abuses involved in the indulgence traffic called into question the unity of the visible church as safeguarded by the papacy. In fact, as we read in this preface,

Luther avers that his own intentions were always peaceable. He did not leave the Roman Catholic Church; he was unjustly excommunicated. He did not found a new church; he restored the old and true church.

But the greatest interest in this preface lies in Luther's account of how he wrestled with Paul's expression "the righteousness of God" in Romans 1:17. This has become controversial again in our own time because of the so-called new perspective on Paul, which either demotes justification to a time-conditioned polemical doctrine or reinterprets it as a cipher for Christian universalism as opposed to Jewish particularism. But these were not Luther's questions. He first took Paul's "righteousness of God" according to the philosophy that prevailed in his day to mean the natural or essential property of God by which God is essentially righteous and by which He righteously judges and punishes the sinful creature. Thinking this way, he reasoned, it is bad enough that in God's law, written on our hearts and enunciated through Moses, the righteous God judges and condemns the unrighteous creature; how much worse, now, if it is all the more reinforced through the gospel, as the meaning seems to be when Paul writes that the "righteousness of God is revealed" through the gospel.

The sense of this interpretation would be something like: Jesus, God incarnate, manifests the natural righteousness of God and by this standard judges the sinful creatures to reward or condemn them. But by studying the usage of the term "righteousness" in the Bible, especially in the Old Testament, Luther slowly broke through to a new understanding. Here righteousness does not designate an inherent and quiescent property of God's nature but expresses God's will in an act revealing God's faithfulness to His own promises. As an act of God's faithfulness, the righteousness of God revealed in the gospel is the Father's giving of the Son into the hands, and yet for the sake, of sinners. As an act of God's faithfulness, the righteousness of God revealed in the gospel is the Son's self-oblation at Gethsemane, the One who came not to be served but to serve and lay down His life as a ransom for many, the One who did not count equality with God a thing to be coveted but emptied and humbled Himself. As an act of

God's faithfulness, the righteousness of God revealed in the gospel is the Spirit's persuasion to faith *pro me* (for me, personally) in the Father's gift and the Son's self-giving. Thus it is the righteousness by which God keeps His promises to make us righteous and holy, asserting His saving reign over and on behalf of the lost and dying creation. It is the "work of God, that is, what God does in us, the power of God, that is, with which he makes us strong, the wisdom of God, with which he makes us wise." Understanding "righteousness" in this new "Hebrew" way, Luther understood why the gospel is good and new and not a refined republication of the law; now the text "the righteousness of God is revealed in the gospel" became for him "truly the gate to paradise" because it pointed to the obedience of Jesus Christ on behalf of the disobedient.

Interestingly, Luther concludes with a note on his relationship to Augustine. "Later," he writes, "I read Augustine's *Spirit and the Letter*, where contrary to hope I found that he, too, had interpreted God's righteousness in a similar way, as the righteousness with which God clothes us when he justifies us." Luther seems to be rewriting history a tad here. Much earlier, in his student days, he had glossed Augustine's great treatise *The City of God* and noted this very teaching by Augustine about gospel righteousness as the divine work and gift that clothes and covers the naked sinner. This is the mature Augustine, who taught that in this life our righteousness for the most part consists in the forgiveness of sins—in other words, the "non-imputation" of sin—and that our actual righteousness in love of God above all and all creatures in and under God is begun, progressing but not finished until the day of the resurrection. Luther's "discovery" of this "Hebrew" sense of the righteousness of God years after his student days, as described in this preface, is thus a recollection, perhaps unconscious, of what he had once learned from Augustine years before but then forgotten. What accounts for this faulty memory, if not doctored recollection, when in those early days Luther's writings are replete with enthusiasm for "the blessed Augustine"?

In the interim, already during the indulgence controversy, Luther discovered that papist opponents could also argue from (the earlier,

more Neoplatonic) Augustine that faith becomes active in love, so
that justifying faith is not faith alone but faith activated by love. Apart
from controversy with papists, however, Luther himself teaches in
exactly the same way, agreeing with the "strawy" Epistle of James
that faith without works is dead and that faith not operative in love
is fraudulent. This is not a contradiction if we bear in mind Luther's
distinction between abstract faith (faith alone in Christ alone justifies) and incarnate faith (faith alone in Christ alone is never alone
but always involves God the Holy Spirit infusing in the believer and
exfusing, so to speak, God's love through the believer to others).

Luther never granted that the reading of his papist opponents was
the correct reading of Augustine, because they made the actual performance of love by the believer, rather than by Christ for the believer,
the ground of righteousness. There is a parallel here to the danger
from Osiander's teaching, which makes the believer's experience of
the inward infusion of grace, rather than the word of Christ predicat-
ing righteousness in the joyful exchange, the ground of justification.
Although here in the preface Luther grudgingly acknowledges that
Augustine "did not explain all things concerning imputation clearly"
(i.e., failing, as we have heard, to regard "imputation" as the abstract
basis of justification, though this criticism of Augustine is anachronistic and thus unfair), Luther also reports how pleased he was to
be reminded that "God's righteousness with which we are justified
was taught" already by Augustine.

I belabor this rather obscure point from the history of theology
because it has much to do with the differentiated consensus on justification achieved in 1999 between the Lutheran World Federation
and the Roman Catholic Church in the Joint Declaration on Justification. Neither Lutherans nor Catholics wish to separate *imputed*
righteousness (that is, the forgiveness that Christ obtains for the helpless sinner given as a gift) from *effective* righteousness (that is, faith
active in love that the Spirit grants as a gift to receive the gift that is
Christ, who transforms the self into a "little Christ" for others). But
within this consensus, they emphasize different poles of the same
dynamic reality.

Misunderstandings of Justification

In the preface to the *Commentary on Galatians* (1535),[8] the mature Luther refined his teaching from the early *Two Kinds of Righteousness* to exposit Christian life as a fundamental receptivity, or patiency, by which God the Creator creates anew to justify sinners and transform believers into agents of Christ's righteousness in the world. In the fifteen years that had transpired since he penned *Two Kinds of Righteousness*, floods of controversy had poured down on Luther from every direction. There was thus a need for a clear and "precise distinction" so that "instructors of conscience" (that is, for Luther, *pastors*) might become adept administrators of God's Word who comfort the afflicted but afflict the comfortable—and know the difference. The need is accentuated because, for Luther, God's Word is, with these diverse effects, something of a living, moving target, a *sic et non* (Yes and No), a comfort or an affliction depending on the context, requiring that ministers administering it become "good dialecticians," who know when to say the Yes of God's gospel to the penitent and when to say the No of God's law to the secure.

Here, then, is that precise distinction that Luther proposes in the preface to his great *Commentary on Galatians*: taken one way, God's Word is law that demands but, just so, by afflicting the auditor with a divine and unconditional demand, reveals bondage to sin and impotence. Taken another way, however, God's Word is good news that just as unconditionally gives what God demands, thus comforting with a promise—namely, Christ the holy friend of sinners, who brings the empowering Holy Spirit to forgive and renew. The difference between God's Word as law and gospel is not in the narrative or ethical content. The Decalogue can be heard as a comforting promise—"I am the LORD your God!"—and the narrative of Christ's passion can be heard as devastating judgment. The difference is rather the perspective from which the ethical or narrative content is articulated, whether as divine and unconditional demand or divine and unconditional promise.

Opposition from outside Luther's own camp seemed at times deliberately to misunderstand his distinction between passive righteousness—that is, Christ's own activated righteousness that we receive as a gift from God—and the active righteousness of such gifted folk who do Christ's works of mercy and justice in the freedom for which Christ has set them free. It is a wooden, if not malicious, misunderstanding to say that Luther rejects the good works of love. They are rejected only as the basis for the justification of the sinner just as they are affirmed as its inevitable consequence. The basis for justification is Christ's good work of love for sinners: Christ alone received by faith alone.

Yet such misunderstanding by opponents had a pretext in the embarrassing fact that among Luther's own followers there was also plenty of misunderstanding. Moreover, Luther's impatience, together with his penchant for exaggerated rhetoric that moves the heart at the expense of careful analysis and patient elaboration that persuades the mind, was partially at fault for misunderstandings within his own camp. We will mention just a few of these intra-Lutheran misunderstandings that are at play in the background of Luther's great attempt to settle the matter in the 1535 *Commentary on Galatians*.

First, the antinomians (the word means "opponents of law") were certain followers of Luther, led by John Agricola, who disowned the Word of God taken as law. These theologians taught the gospel only and thought that retaining the Word of God as law was a lapse back into Judaism (a smear against Catholicism that unfortunately persists to this day). By that very token, they thought that the law itself is not really God's own Word but rather a human word and a human tradition. Law is nothing, then, but Jewish legalism based on the wrathful depiction of God in the Old Testament. Such was the teaching of the "gospel alone" theologians who did away with the holy demand of God, as Creator to creature, and who instead wanted to preach only grace.

But grace too suffers a definite deformation under the antinomians. Grace ceases to be grace for sinners—those guilty under the law—and becomes grace for the victims of human legalism. Grace is not taken as the costly Word of God incarnate for us at Calvary that surpasses and triumphs over another word of God that stood against us as sinners. Rather, for the antinomians, grace becomes the Christian idea of God, the Christian principle, the Christian religious insight into the niceness of God. This cheap grace of the antinomians, as Dietrich Bonhoeffer diagnosed it in *The Cost of Discipleship*, is the "Lutheran" heresy.[9]

In the Galatians commentary Luther has to attend to the difference between a false opinion about the law as a way to righteousness before God (that would be "legalism," Jewish or otherwise) and the true sense of the law as God at work as the holy Judge showing us our need for a righteousness that goes beyond the law to give us, precisely, what we do not deserve according to the law.

A second front that had arisen within Luther's own camp was formed by the followers of Andreas Osiander, of whom we have already heard. Osiander interpreted the righteousness of God given in the gospel as an infusion (like an injection of medicine) into the soul. This medicine is the righteousness by which God is naturally righteous—that is, a divine and supernatural quality that, as it were, burns away our sinfulness and smelts us into righteousness. Osiander's followers were the kind of "born again" theologians who turn the promise of God, received in Spirit-worked faith and conforming us to Christ's death and resurrection, into the religious experience of being overwhelmed and changed causally by an occult power. Luther in the Galatians commentary, then, had to spell out how the righteousness of God in Christ is not God's natural property, now supernaturally infused into creatures and causing something like a chemical reaction in the depths of their souls, but rather God's amazing decision and deed of loving His enemies in the mission, passion, and vindication of His incarnate Son, reorganizing human affects head to toe when it strikes home in the power of the Spirit.

The third misunderstanding is the most difficult and subtle, because it was the misunderstanding of Luther's closest friend and comrade-in-arms, Philipp Melanchthon. Melanchthon was so disturbed by the implication of ethical permissiveness in the antinomian

position, and so concerned that Osiander's view of infused righteousness gave away the store to Roman Catholic opponents who
wanted to base justification on the believer's moral renewal and
progress, that he overreacted on both fronts. And this overreaction
is what ever since has been typically known as *the* Lutheran position
on justification.

Against the antinomians, Melanchthon held that God's law is
eternal, the standard of righteousness rooted in the divine and immutable nature of God. The gospel therefore must be taken as a
supplementary aid, a jerry-rigged contraption devised after the fall
for attaining to this divine and immutable standard, which Christ
achieved instead of us by his perfect legal obedience and now applies
gratuitously to those who believe, provided that they take that small
but definite step of accepting it (he called this baby step of the human
will the third factor in justification because it finally decides between
the saved and the damned). Moreover, those who do so believe must
then demonstrate the authenticity of their belief by striving to fulfill
the law, which provides a guide for their lives—the so-called third use
of the law. In this way, law becomes the eternal Word of God and
the gospel an ad hoc supplement to it. And the Holy Spirit becomes
no more than a gloss on the "human response" to God's grace. And
Christ is away, up in heaven, having attainted the treasury of merit
now available for imputation to the sinner who decides to accept it.
All this depiction of justification, ironically, is far closer to Anselm
of Canterbury than to Martin Luther!

Against Osiander, Melanchthon taught that God's grace is not a
supernatural power that is infused into the soul but a divine attitude
of favor that credits ("imputes") Christ's merit from His keeping of
the law to the sinful creature who does not and cannot keep the law.
Then, and only then, with the guilty and indebted sinner's account
put in balance by the application of Christ's merit, does God send the
Spirit to renew the sinful creature, who in turn strives to demonstrate
that she is worthy of this accreditation.

What's wrong with Melanchthon's view from the perspective of the
mature Luther, who also rejects the misunderstandings of Agricola

and Osiander? As is taught in Galatians 3, for Luther the law is temporary. It is the promise of God that is eternal. The law, then, is a servant of the gospel, not the gospel a servant of the law. Reversing this, Melanchthon's scheme unwittingly destroys Christian freedom and puts believers back under the law, where they must strive to demonstrate that they are worthy of grace. Even worse, from all that we have learned about Luther's joyful exchange in this chapter, the presence of Jesus Christ and the work of the Holy Spirit are reduced to mere figures of speech that do nothing in the present, according to this scheme. What Christ did once and for all in the past is present only as a memory. What makes a Christian is not the Holy Spirit's effective election here and now calling forth and empowering faith, but that tiny little step of personal choice where one accepts the good deal of Christ's merit traded in exchange for sin.

For Luther, it is the living and present Christ in the *free* and *joyful*, not legal or commercial, exchange who one-sidedly announces the promise, "I am yours and you are mine," who accordingly commands with the authority of the new creation, "Give me your sin and take my righteousness." And for Luther, it is the Spirit's gift of faith that empowers the believer to do just this, giving up sin and "taking hold" of Christ in His promise. Because God now sees the believer "wrapped" in Christ by Spirit-given faith, God does not "impute" the sin that remains (and must remain as long as we live in the body and by the body stay organically connected to the structures of malice and injustice that prevail on this good earth until the kingdom comes). In short, Melanchthon turns Luther's wedding feast into a courtroom transaction.

More precisely, Luther and Melanchthon differ subtly on the technical matter of "imputation," or biblically, on "reckoning," as in Romans 4:22. For Luther, God reckons faith in Christ as righteousness before Him to the one to whom faith in Christ has been given as a gift by the Spirit. As a result, whether viewed from the objective pole of Christ's gift or the subjective pole of the Spirit working faith, it is all and always God's grace that takes the initiative and completes the good work so begun. At the bottom of things for Luther is the

Spirit, who sovereignly blows where He will, calling to faith as He proclaims the righteousness of Christ.

For Melanchthon, Luther's reference to the Holy Spirit's gift of faith to receive the gift of Christ seemed too close for comfort to Osiander's idea of the infusion of grace into the soul. Luther's speech of Christ present and active in the joyful exchange, moreover, sounded similar to the antinomian claim that the gospel alone, without the law, works all in all. So Melanchthon eventually dismissed the joyful exchange—the christological heart of Luther's teaching on justification—as a merely decorative "way of talking," not a real "way of being." At bottom for Melanchthon, then, is the little human act of will that accepts the good deal offered by God. It is that—not the Holy Spirit's election—which accounts for the justified in distinction from those not justified.

The end result for Melanchthon is the familiar but incoherent scheme known as Lutheran "forensic" righteousness: God the heavenly Judge applies the infinite merit of Christ to the terrified sinner who, traumatized by life's woe and a bad conscience, cries out for mercy. Or, if people are not already traumatized by life, preachers have to provide motivation by terrorizing sinners so that they can appreciate the good deal of pardon proffered in the gospel.

The changes are subtle but have massive implications. How far we have traveled here from the gospel as Christ's unilateral and joyful exchange of His good for our evil, giving nothing less than His Spirit to engender faith in exchange for our despair! What a change in scheme to a static world—in which individuals are confronted with an eternal standard to which they must conform lest they suffer the eternal pains of hell—from Luther's apocalyptic world, in which God's justice is on the march through the gospel to win back the suffering creation for His reign! What a subtle but disastrous confusion that makes preachers into rhetorical terrorists before they can ever announce the gospel with its tidings of comfort and joy! What a failure, then, that does not and cannot provide insightful interpretations of the actual terror that desperate people—today more than ever—hopelessly hold at bay with idols and demons!

With the preceding remarks, readers are equipped to read between the lines of Luther's preface to his great *Commentary on Galatians*, hopefully inspired by that to go on and excavate the many gems found in the commentary itself: the *vita passiva* (the "passive life") of receptivity, permission, taking hold of the gift that Christ is that lets God be God also "for me"; the therapy that pastors practice as "instructors of conscience"; the dynamic interpretation of the *simul iustus et peccator* (at the same time righteous and sinner) as a personalization of the apocalyptic battle of the old world dying and the new creation arising; Christ the Victor, a savior not a legislator; the *baptizatus sum* (I am baptized) of faith, which is the sure foundation, not the uncertain goal, of Christian life; the concrete reference of theological language to what God is doing in the world "to make and keep human life human" (Paul Lehmann), rather than ethereal flights of language into a poetry of what cannot be known; the clarity that law with its commandments is given for the sake of the neighbor in need, so that the Sabbath was made for humanity, not humanity for the Sabbath; the further clarity that the law of love for God as for others is the true, inescapable, and holy demand of God as Creator to creature that must be satisfied and surpassed if there is to be peace with God; and the final clarity that peace with God is achieved by God and given, even to failures before that holy law, in Christ the Lamb, who takes away the sin of the world.

New Birth by the Spirit

The new birth by the Spirit unites the believer with the Son as recipient of the Father's favor and as agent in Christ of the Father's glory. Following Augustine, Luther thinks of the Holy Spirit as the bond of love between the Father and the Son, who now includes creatures in this bonding of the Beloved Community, which the Holy Trinity primordially is. The Holy Spirit persuades by shedding God's love abroad in our hearts—a persuasion that is rational in the sense that its reason is Jesus Christ, but is not rationalistic. Overcoming human mistrust of God at the very seat of human desire in the "heart," itself scarred and warped by the sinful dynamics of the fallen creation, is not chiefly a matter of theoretical or philosophical doubts. Such doubts can be important and demand theological attention. But only the Spirit's actual communication of love remedies Adam's mistrust. That remedy is what the Spirit works in every sermon and ceremony and fellowship by presenting Jesus Christ as the deed of God's love, even for the enemy that I am as a sinner despairing of love.

Thus Luther's explanation of the third article of the Creed begins emphatically with the confession, "I believe that by my own understanding or strength I cannot believe in Jesus Christ my Lord or come to Him, but instead the Holy Spirit has called me through the gospel, enlightened me with his gifts, made me holy and kept me in the true faith, just as he calls, gathers, enlightens, and makes holy the whole Christian church on earth and keeps it with Jesus Christ in the one common, true faith." Here daily the Spirit is at work forgiving sins until at last the Spirit raises to eternal life. Article 5 of the Augsburg Confession echoes this strong theology of the Spirit when it speaks of God working through Word and sacrament to give the Holy Spirit—that is, "as through means to create faith where and when it pleases God."

In his Christmas hymn "From Heaven Above to Earth I Come,"[10] Luther immortalized this understanding of faith as the Spirit's new birth. Luther's Christmas sermons generally are replete with the exhortation "It does you no good that Christ was born in Bethlehem unless He is born anew today in you." By this Luther distinguished a merely historical faith that Christ was born in Bethlehem from the justifying faith of personal appropriation and trust that, as such, reorganizes human affects. Thus the climax of this hymn comes in verse 13, with the prayer to the Christ-child that He would today be born anew into "my" heart (see appendix). This prayer expresses the important principle that justifying faith is personal trust, *fiducia*, that receives Christ personally, "for me."

This Christmas hymn is dated to around 1535, when Luther's own children would have been old enough for singing the Christian faith into their young hearts. The scholarly conjecture is that the hymn originated in Luther's family devotion, with the parents singing the part of the angels in verses 1–5, individual children singing verses 8–14, and all together singing verses 7 and 15. Luke's depiction of the angels' proclamation of the good news to the shepherds structures the first part. Thus the parents lead the children to sing their parts to the Christ-child by concluding the introductory verses with the exhortation of the shepherds in verse 6 to "draw near / to see the wondrous Gift of God." The hymn concludes with all voices joining the angels in the praise of God.

The gospel promise and the narrative of the Bible go together. The reason why is that the world is full of promises, as mentioned above. Augustus Caesar on his imperial throne also makes promises: to be benefactor and peacemaker. Caesar claims to be the incarnation of God's rule on the earth. But Luke's Christmas narrative identifies another king, not like Caesar, without "velvets soft and silken stuff," a newborn asleep on "hay and straw so rough." At this surprising discovery of the shepherds in Bethlehem, Luther is filled with childlike wonder at the humility of the one true God set against the arrogance of His proud creature. Luther's hymn thus invites us to become little children again in love and adoration.

Paul said it first, that "though he was rich, yet for your sakes he became poor" (2 Cor. 8:9), and John made it the chief principle of Christian theology: "The Word became flesh and lived among us, . . . full of grace and truth" (John 1:14). The patristic theology of the early Catholic Church focused on this wonder of the condescension of God in the philanthropy of the Logos, who became what we are in order that we might become what He is, as Irenaeus and Athanasius put it. Augustine loved again and again to contrast the pride of the creature who wants to be god without God with the humility of the God who will not be God without us, even us in our desperate and harmful arrogance. Luther captures all this doxological wonder of the church fathers at the *admirabile commercium*, the "joyful exchange," when he has us sing with the children, "O Lord, you have created all! How did you come to be so small?" *Admirabile commercium*! An astonishing exchange!

Unlike philosophical theology, which is embarrassed at the condescension of God and finds in the incarnation of the Son of God the
nonsense of a contradiction rather than the paradox of a love that
knows no bounds, Luther's theology of the biblical narrative knows
God deep in the flesh—or not at all. Just so, we should firmly note
Luther's virtual equation of the Holy Spirit and the gift of justifying
faith. "Faith" is Luther's word for the Holy Spirit given and at work
in the new birth of human beings so that what the Word promises
and gives can be truly heard and personally appropriated. Just as
Ernst Käsemann used to say that justification is Paul the apostle's
"applied Christology," we could likewise say that faith is Luther's
"applied theology of the Holy Spirit." It is quite a bitter irony, then,
if it sometimes seems as if *this* Holy Spirit has disappeared from
Lutheranism![11]

There is a reason for that. Though two, they belong together: the
incarnate Word, witnessed in Scripture and proclaimed in Word and
sacrament, and the Holy Spirit, given through the Word in order to
create the faith to receive the Word. The Son is given by the Spirit,
and the Spirit is given by the Son, one by another and never the one
without the other, yet always in this back-and-forth between two who
are personally distinct yet essentially related.

But in Lutheran history, and more generally Protestant history,
this applied trinitarian theology—which distinguishes the really distinct persons of the incarnate Word and the Spirit and at the same
time relates them essentially and thus inseparably to each other in
their mutually reinforcing operations—faded from consciousness. In
Protestant orthodoxy, the Word alone was thought to be given in the
miraculously guaranteed inspiration of the Scriptures. The emphasis
on the objectivity of the Word in the Bible was so pronounced that
the human reception of the Word in the Spirit's grant of justifying
faith was practically neglected, as the father of German Pietism,
Philipp Jakob Spener, lamented in his *Pia Desideria*.

Lutheran Pietism, which had parallels in Reformed and Anglican
Protestantism, reacted against this pastorally disastrous neglect in
the name of the objectivity of the Bible and the monergism of grace.

As opposed to the "head knowledge" of the theologians, the experience of the reception of the Word in the new birth took increasing precedence over the specific form given to faith by the incarnate Word. Eventually, any "spiritual" experience became the main thing, no matter how distantly related to the cross and resurrection of the incarnate Word.[12] Orthodoxy thus anticipates modern fundamentalism while Pietism anticipates modern liberalism. Both separate and indeed antagonize what Luther held together in lifting up the person and work of the Holy Spirit as the Spirit of the Father and the Son.

It is fascinating to see how Luther also holds personal and corporate experience together in a way that corresponds to this trinitarian unity in difference of the Word and the Spirit. The contemporary alienation between "spirituality" and "organized religion" is totally alien to Luther's theology of the Spirit, who works on each person personally precisely by gathering each one into "mother Church," where the Word is proclaimed and experienced rightly in the gospel-gathered fellowship of mutual love.

There are two reasons why Luther can hold personal and corporate experience together. First, Luther rejects strong notions of individual agency. He denies that "by my own understanding or strength" anyone can find the way to the merciful Savior, Jesus Christ, let alone climb up to God almighty without Him. In contemporary language, we might say that, for Luther, individuals are not autonomous subjects or sovereigns but social patients, whose agency in the world is always a function of those greater powers to which they yield themselves as persons, whether in the final analysis as puppets of Satan or as beloved children of the heavenly Father. Thus, I can only be a human person in relation to something other and greater than myself, in whose agency I find my own true power and mission in life. In this way my personal experience and my social or corporate world go together, even if a new kind of conflict between the old life in Adam and the new life in Christ overlays this personal-social self.

Second, like his teacher Augustine, Luther holds that we are moved in all things by our loves. He rejects as a rationalistic fiction the belief that human beings are properly identified by the capacity of calculating reason and that their worth accordingly depends on governing themselves successfully according to reason's enlightened self-interest. For howsoever "enlightened," at bottom this remains self-interest, self-love. But our salvation from sin and for beloved community consists in loving God above all and all creatures in and under God. Jesus Christ is the One who so loved, so that our salvation consists in His love for us and His love in us. Thus, for Luther, human beings are properly identified in Jesus Christ as beloved children of His heavenly Father, and their worth accordingly is given as the gift of the Holy Spirit in the assurance of forgiveness and the power to live new life.

As human creatures we are motivated in everything we do by our loves. The real issue in life, according to Luther, is what we love and whether it is truly worthy of all our love. This vision of the human reality and the human predicament is deeply at odds with modern ideas of the sovereign self, the debased image of which in our culture is the consumer, whose joy in life is to choose between equally superfluous toys. The work of the Holy Spirit is to present to us a crucified Jewish male of the first century and to ask us whether we find anything attractive about Him. What a stumbling block! When we have turned our heads away in repugnance from this sight, then, and only then, are we in the place where the revelation of the Lamb of God who takes away the sin of the world—and also mine—can be spoken, heard, and believed. Such is the new birth from above.

2

The Bible

THERE ARE "MANY WORDS FROM GOD." Even the Bible has "many words from God." This was a key objection from papist opponents. How can you claim the authority of Scripture when Scripture says so many diverse things? Interestingly, this is the same objection we hear more and more today from deconstructionist critics, who assure us of the ambiguity of biblical texts with their multiple layers of crisscrossing meanings. As Brad S. Gregory has shown, neglect of this serious objection would lead future Protestants down the rabbit hole of pursuing a supernaturally self-clarifying Bible but in reality producing thousands of Protestant sects, each claiming for itself the one true and plain-sense meaning of the Bible. But after acknowledging the prima facie objection to his appeal to the Bible rightly read, Luther already specified that the Word of God is, following Romans 1:2–4, the Father's "gospel concerning his Son," as Luther put it in his treatise *The Freedom of the Christian*. It is this message of the resurrection of the Crucified that has reached out from Israel to all nations and made us believers. The gospel in turn is our access to the Scriptures and key to their interpretation. That is the theme of this chapter.

Interpreting the Bible

Much of contemporary evangelicalism was birthed during the Enlightenment and formed by its demand for a foundational knowledge of knowledge. "Foundationalism" and "epistemology" are names for this pursuit. This pursuit took the Latin slogan *sola scriptura* as an epistemological or foundational principle rather than in the instrumental way (the Latin is in the ablative case!) that Luther presumed—namely, that the Scriptures are the Spirit's means of sanctifying readers by providing access to the historical sources of the gospel. We can illustrate the difference this made within German church history with the rise of Pietism, a phenomenon that parallels the rise of evangelicalism in Anglo-American lands, by considering the conversion of August Hermann Francke (1663–1727).

R. W. Meyer points out that "there is little in common between Francke's and Luther's experience of the religious crisis."[1] Luther sought assurance of grace for the troubled penitent. Francke, as an orthodox Lutheran, affirmed this doctrine of grace. But Francke had lost the immediate and personal experience of this love. It was for Francke "a lifeless formula," compensated by "his anxious insistence upon 'the act and reality of faith,'" as if in this way to will faith into existence. It becomes clear that "the religious dilemma becomes identical with an intellectual dilemma unknown to Luther." What was this new dilemma? "When, in his spiritual anguish, Francke turned to the Bible, it occurred to him 'to wonder whether the Scriptures are truly the Word of God. Do not the Turks make this claim on behalf of their Koran, and the Jews on behalf of the Talmud? And who shall say who is right?'"[2] Francke worries more about historical relativism than a gracious God. But what is decisive is that Francke's "breakthrough" was not Luther's new conviction about the righteousness of God given as a gift in the person of Christ through faith, but "the assurance of man's knowledge of God, the validity of the Bible and of the Christian tradition."[3] Supernatural assurance of the validity of the Bible overcame Francke's doubts, and just this, he felt, was his own experience of the new birth.

It is certainly the case that the Bible is our access to the historic event of Christ and thus to knowledge of the God of the gospel. But it is this access to *us*—that is, to us gentiles to whom the gospel has first come and gathered, evoking faith. In this important way we specify the hermeneutical or interpretative relationship to the Bible. That access is the community of faith to which the Spirit brings us, there to preach the gospel from the Scriptures. It is not by way of a supernaturally guaranteed revelation of a perfect being in a perfect text overcoming epistemological doubts (a notion that corresponds better to Muhammad's claim for the Qur'an than the Genesis-to-Revelation canon of the Christian tradition). In fact, Francke's resolution to his doubts about the validity of the Bible as alone valid in comparison to all other religious texts was to suppress legitimate questions about the historical interpretation of the Bible itself. And this act of suppressing inquiry handed that inquiry over to those who proclaimed their scientific freedom from religiously imposed restraints on their research. According to Molly Worthen, as we noted at the outset of this book, this attempt to cordon off the Bible from historical inquiry by means of a doctrine of inerrancy has virtually collapsed today, leading to a crisis of fundamentals in evangelicalism. But here Luther's gospel approach to the interpretation of Scripture can really help since it can in a principled way distinguish between the treasure and the earthen vessel that bears it.

Luther's approach can also liberate the precious new birth and the fullness of conviction that it brings from Francke's false association of it with epistemological foundationalism. The gospel is gospel not simply as news. It is news, of course, but to believe this news would be only a historical faith, such as also the demons possess—even if assurance that the report is true were a matter of supernatural experience in the new birth that worked to suppress doubts. This historical news could be, in Luther's understanding, also nothing but a demand of the law, as we shall see in chapter 4 when we study Luther's *Meditation on Christ's Passion*. As historical report, the mere news that Christ died innocently for our sins rather "terrifies" the "natural man" who does not yet know and trust that this sinless death was for the good of the sinner. The historical report is not yet good news for me, the sinner. Rather, the gospel is good news when this news that Christ died for our sins becomes the event "for me" of God's self-donation for my sake, out of boundless mercy surpassing His own law's just demand and thus also surpassing my failure before God in order to embrace me like the lost sheep the shepherd has sought and found to carry home.

In his commentary on Psalm 23:2,[4] Luther exposits the green pastures and the still waters of this much-loved psalm as similitudes of the Word and the sacraments that constitute the Christian community in the gospel and keep the flock safe and well nourished through its sojourn. The "meaning of the whole psalm," Luther tells us, is "that whoever has the Lord as a Shepherd will not want." That is the literal sense of the metaphor of green pasture and still waters—in other words, the cognitive claim being made about something in the world. So, Luther continues, the psalm "does not teach anything more" than this divine supply of true needs; it only in various ways emphasizes "the thought further by means of fine figurative words and pictures," showing how those who have the Lord as a Shepherd want for nothing and are rather satisfied. "See how beautifully [the psalm] can speak!"

Understanding Metaphor

However, before we come to the provision of the Lord in the table spread for our nourishment in Word and sacrament, as Luther expounds, it is well to meditate a little on these initial comments about literal reference and figurative words or word pictures. For there is a great deal of confusion today about what is literal and what is metaphorical.

"With what can we compare the rise of metaphor in recent theology, or what parable shall we use to describe it? It is like the kudzu plant, which begins as one sprout among many, but ends up hiding everything under its smothering embrace."[5] With this humorous parody of Mark 4:30–32, the contemporary Methodist theologian R. Kendall

Soulen, in an important book, spells out the problem of contemporary confusion. He traces the root of the doctrine of the Trinity in the Old Testament's knowledge of the God of the exodus, "who will cause His Name [the Father] to be remembered, to come [the Son] and to bless [the Spirit]" (Exod. 20:24, trans. Soulen). Because this saving God is the One whom we are talking about, none of our usual metaphors capture Him, bound as they are to our experience in this fallen world. Rather, the Spirit has given us certain, definite "forms of speech" especially in the creeds, so Luther maintains,[6] that point to the One "who causes His Name to be remembered, to come and to bless." We don't have God by pronouncing a name. But God has us when He causes His name to be remembered so that He can come and bless.

For Luther, the God of the Bible is the One who is incomparable and thus essentially incomprehensible, as Isaiah teaches at the climax of his preaching (Isa. 55:8–9); we worldlings, however, only understand by way of comparisons that inch forward with analogies from the greater known to the lesser known within a world fallen into malice and injustice, blind to its own true plight. But the one true God is not part of the world, whether we regard Him as greater known or lesser known. God is qualitatively other, Creator not creature, the one true God who alone can truly save. As Isaiah goes on to teach, then, we can *only* know God truly as Creator and Redeemer who brings about the new creation by virtue of His own initiative (grace alone) and His self-communicating Word (Christ alone; cf. Isa. 55:11), apprehended by Spirit-given faith alone from the Scriptures alone. Just so, faith knows in whom it believes; it understands enough to follow in the obedience of faith; and in hope it believes that belief shall give way to sight, the light of grace shining in the darkness giving way to the unending daylight of glory.

Notice, then, that reverence and respect for the essential mysteriousness of God our Creator and the Savior of all comes not as a natural insight but as a gift given with the advent of knowledge of God by the light of grace. In recent times, however, it has been something of a theological fad to claim knowledge of God's incomparability by way of the light of nature rather than the light of grace. John Hick, Paul Knitter, and James Cobb speak for many when they affirm in various ways that there is a mysterious and transcendent reality that has only partially revealed itself in each of the various religious traditions, so that the normative claims of each tradition are due to human narrow-mindedness and not to the validity of any of the claims.[7] In this theology, the light of nature eclipses the light of grace! For Luther, such theology turns things Christian upside down. It merely reverts to pre-Christian Platonism. It makes the "natural man" (1 Cor. 2:14) into the one who knows God in glorious ineffability, God beyond the gods, just as it makes the theologian of the cross, who knows God in the visibility of the Crucified, into the fool who thinks to capture God in theological forms of speech. But just this paradox of the incomparable God giving Himself for sinful creatures is what the apostle Paul claimed when he proclaimed "Christ crucified," the folly of God wiser than the wisdom of humans. Who really better respects the mystery of God?

What an enormous difference this makes! By the light of reasoning from comparisons within our experience of the world, theologians of glory, as Luther termed those who thought they were already in heaven, become at length exhausted with the failure of any speech to represent God and thus come to the negative conclusion that God is infinite, beyond, unknowable, unlike anything here and now. And this ignorance of God they claim as insight into God! Because they arrive at this negative conclusion that none of our worldly words, concepts, and images can capture or contain the infinite, they are put into the position of acknowledging that all our "metaphors" for God are nothing but our own projections. None of them are, or can be, literally true. None correspond adequately to the infinite reality to which they point. They fail as representations and are reduced to empty signs substituting for the thing signified, which is absent.

Manifestly, this is a very bad result for Christian theology, at the center of which is the incarnation, the coming of the Word of God in the flesh, and Pentecost, the coming of the messianic Spirit to "call, gather, and enlighten" faith by the mission of the church to all nations. Yet this bad result is necessary medicine, so the argument of today's "mainline" theologians of glory goes, to arrest in its tracks Christian fundamentalism, which, it is alleged, idolatrously takes the metaphors literally.

Thus we are to suppose, I suppose, that "fundamentalists," upon hearing the psalm's petition "Hide me in the shadow of your wings," insist that God is a large chicken. This overwrought critique of fundamentalism is little more than a caricature of an enemy that has been culturally defeated since the evolution controversies of the 1920s. It reappears as little more than a bogeyman smearing today's evangelicals and Pentecostals, with whom, to be sure, Luther's kind of theology has certain issues, as we are presently exploring.

In any event, self-described "metaphorical theologians" remedy the disillusionment that their negative theology works—but by *not* recommending the Bible as a Spirit-inspired source for our gospel theology (the "pure, clear fountain of Israel," as second-generation Lutheran reformers put it), giving knowledge of God from God by God. According to this ultimately agnostic theology, the Bible is *not* authoritative because God has spoken by delivering Israel from Egypt and raising Jesus His Son from the grave and exalting Him as the coming Lord of the cosmos, to which Word of God incarnate the Bible attests, where and when the Spirit blesses with faith. Rather, they argue, the Bible provides a *pattern* for contemporary metaphor making. The need, so they argue, is for metaphors today as liberating as the ones Jesus is alleged to have spoken (but recall: his liberating metaphors got Him crucified), following the *pattern* of His speech, to tell us what God is like in liberating ways. This is the result: whatever liberates is thus biblical, while the Bible itself can say or claim nothing that is actually true about God. We are to speak as humans in the *pattern* of the Bible, not in the *terms* of the Bible as humans led by the Spirit of Jesus Christ. What this view does not acknowledge is that it is only by speaking in the terms of the Bible that we remain anchored in the historical Christ event. We do not translate terms like "Abba," "Messiah/Christ," "Jesus," or "Israel." We transliterate them. If we translated them, we would transform them from names into ciphers.

So this contemporary line of argument is quite confused. Metaphors have a literal meaning or they are just nonsense. As I often illustrate to my students: if I said to my beloved, "Fly to me on the wings of your love," and if she, under the passion of her desire, were to climb to the roof of the building, right up to the top, and leap into the sky, expecting the sheer power of our eros to fuel her flight into my waiting arms, she would have lethally misunderstood my metaphor. Janet Soskice makes the same point with another humorous example. "Don't touch the wire. It's live!" someone might say. If I were to reply, "That's only a metaphor. It is not literally alive," and then confidently grasp that wire, I would be literally, not metaphorically, electrocuted. The wire is literally electrified, and that literal truth is expressed by the metaphor "live wire."[8]

This is how Luther thinks about the Bible. Biblical interpretation is a matter of discerning the literal sense of the comparative metaphor, the similitude, how it makes sense by referring to something in the world by comparing a lesser known to a greater known. If such metaphors are not seen to refer to something in the world, all one is left with is a collage of suggestive words and allusive images shifting like a kaleidoscope—not a bad description, by the way, of some contemporary theology that has learned deconstruction but not yet reconstruction! But taken in Soskice's "literal" way, let us look at the fruit that this method of interpretation yields in Luther's exposition of Psalm 23:2.

Metaphor and the Church

Luther's commentary on Psalm 23:2 yields a pretty timely critique of the "prosperity gospel" that has captivated some TV preachers and megachurch hucksters. "We, too," Luther writes, "should learn this art, namely, to let the world glory forever in great riches, honor, and power. For these are indeed loose, uncertain, perishable wares that God lets men scramble for. . . . To His children, however, as David says here, He gives the genuine treasure." How important it is for Luther that preachers, today more than ever, preach prophetic critiques of

our rampant envy and regnant greed, beginning at home within the
religion business, to all the more proclaim the imperative, "Seek first
the reign of God and its righteousness," with its promise, "and all
these things shall be added unto you!"

This critique requires preachers to present our Lord Jesus Christ
as the true object of desire. He, Luther writes, is the "pearl of great
price, . . . sure and eternal and better than all worldly possessions."
We find this pearl, moreover, in the green pasture that is "God's
people and the Holy Christian Church." Here God "commits to the
Holy Christian Church the office of a shepherd, entrusts and gives to
it the holy Gospel and sacraments, so that by means of these it may
care for and watch over His sheep, and so that these sheep may be
richly provided with instruction, comfort, strength and protection
against all evil."

In all these ways, Luther discerns interpretively the literal sense of
the psalm's metaphors: it is the foretaste of the Beloved Community
that is the congregation gathered to Word and sacrament. Further,
Luther focuses on this gift: the Good Shepherd gives to the community under-shepherds—"pastors," as we might say—who care for the
flock of God not with rules and regulations, as if they were jurists,
but as pastors guiding and feeding the flock with the holy gospel and
its sacraments. Sometimes Luther's teaching of the priesthood of all
believers is mistaken as teaching that each individual can be priest
for himself or herself. This is not the same as Luther's meaning but
its opposite!

First, for Luther, *all* the baptized are priests—that is to say, not
for themselves but *for others*, "little Christs to the neighbor in need,"
as we will learn in the next chapter when we study *The Freedom of
a Christian*. Thus all the people of God in their secular stations are
summoned to transform these worldly stations, tasks, and duties into
holy secularity, vocations of Christian service.

Second, of these baptized people, some are called and ordained to
minister *to* the Word and the sacraments so that the law and gospel of
God are spoken well and aptly, just as Luther describes the office of
the pastor above—namely, to see to the performance of the life-giving

means of grace for the sake of making and keeping the community in Christ Christian.

Third, of the baptized people, some others may be commissioned *from* the Word and sacraments to perform works of justice and mercy on behalf of the local body in its parish or neighborhood. Thus you have the general priesthood, the pastoral office of Word and sacrament, and diaconal ministries. How much heartache and confusion of expectations in congregational life we have experienced because we do not pay attention to such important distinctions!

In my view, we could add to this list a genuine ministry of oversight that serves the true unity of the local congregations with others in the doctrine of the gospel, a pastor of pastors and congregations. We can do this also in Luther's name, because when the bishops of Germany withheld ministry from territories adopting the Reformation, Luther and his colleagues undertook the special duties of the bishop in visitation, supervision, and ordination. Because the bishops of his day were feudal lords who neglected their Christian duty to ordain pastors where the Reformation had been adopted in Germany, the official episcopal system was suspended and resort was taken to the secular princes as "emergency bishops" who financed and legally regulated such "episcopal" supervision. In time this arrangement led to the notorious obsequiousness of the German Lutheran regional churches to the secular authorities.

For us today, long after the disestablishment of Protestantism, a genuinely ecclesial form of churchly self-government could emerge from a renewal of episcopacy. But then, if we were really serious about that, we would not impose term limits when we call our overseers— that is, our "bishops"—just as we do not impose term limits on congregational pastors. Moreover, we would give them the corresponding power to instruct, comfort, strengthen, and protect against wandering from the flock and straying from the path of the gospel mission to the nations by asking them and expecting them to be our local theologians, apt in teaching the Word. Then they would be bishops literally, not metaphorically—in reality, not only in name (however gussied up with croziers and pectoral crosses and purple shirts).

Needless to say, in all such offices persons are held accountable to the duties with which they are entrusted, and the people of God, for Luther, have the right and duty to judge their performance by the standard of God's Word, as Jesus says in John 10:27: "My sheep hear my voice. I know them, and they follow me." But we elect pastors and bishops today like politicians, as if the church were a political democracy rather than a holy community. Why are we disappointed when they act like politicians? We hire and fire pastors like employees. Why are we disappointed when they act like the overworked and underpaid employees that they are? We do not honor congregational ministers to the community as deacons. Why are we disappointed when they cease to appreciate the Christian source and nature of their service in the gospel?

If we were to take Luther's way of deciphering biblical metaphor for its sense in such literal references in the world, perhaps we would today get far more meaning from the Bible than we are prepared for! That very manner of decipherment, I venture, is what made Luther into a change agent in his own day and could still do so in ours.

Biblical Authority

We see here, then, an important sample of what the authority of the Bible is for Luther and how it actually works to author and authorize personal trust in corporate life. What the Bible essentially is for Luther is a promissory narrative—that is, a story that presents Jesus Christ in such a way that His promise to be with us and for us is intelligible and thus trustworthy. When we can so identify Jesus Christ by biblical narrative, we can hear *His* personal promise, "I am yours and you are mine," and distinguish it from imposters and frauds. This is a very necessary discrimination. The world is full of false prophets and false messiahs promising us that we can have our cake and eat it too. But the Spirit's *Holy* Scripture works by presenting and urging Jesus Christ (*was Christum treibet*), who gives life to those who spiritually die with Him. This presentation of Jesus Christ that we may die and rise with Him is the "spiritual" authority of the Bible—in the sense that the Holy Spirit uses this specific ("canonical") narrative to bring Christ to us and us to Christ.

It is not, then, that the Bible is authoritative because it formally possesses divine and supernatural qualities (like being "inerrant") and therefore gives needed but otherwise inaccessible information about God by means of a special miracle of inspiration. That is how, as mentioned above, Muslims think about the authority of the holy Qur'an. Indeed, the word "Qur'an" means "recitation"—in other words, Muhammad's strict and unadulterated recording of the very words miraculously given to him so that, as he thought, unlike Jewish and Christian Scripture, the words of the Qur'an would not be "corrupted" by human additions. Ironically, this dictation theory of scriptural authority entered the Christian West through the medieval encounter with Islam and was unconsciously adopted by later Protestants to back up their antipapal epistemological claims, as if to say, "We don't need an inerrant teaching office in the pope since we have an inerrant Bible."

Such authoritarian thinking reflects a strange alienation from what Luther found unique and irreplaceable about the Bible. Thinking to honor the Bible, dictation theory makes the Bible as such the foundation of faith. It makes the true content of the Bible in the Spirit's hands through present proclamation in Word and sacrament—namely, Christ as saving Lord—secondary to the formal authority of a supposed supernatural revelation. As a result, it effectively consigns the Holy Spirit to past history in the original inspiration of the Bible and in the process makes everything in the Bible of equal authority and relevance. But Luther does not think we can either perceive or receive the gift of Christ from the Scriptures apart from the Holy Spirit, who speaks to us today through the specific human witness of the biblical writers taken up by present-day preachers to give faith where and when it pleases God. Luther uses the nativity image of the manger crib of the Christ-child to illustrate: the Bible is the manger in which we find Christ. Of course, this manger is indispensable. Without it we cannot have Christ in the world, but with and through it Christ becomes present to us. Thus the Bible has the Spirit's authority, the authority to author and authorize faith, to make auditors holy. The Spirit speaks through the human words and witness of the prophets and the apostles to tell of Christ and in this particular way to speak God's promises through Him to us.

God's Mercy and Human Sin

Another way to think about the Scripture principle comes with the realization that the Genesis-to-Revelation canon is a great narrative of the world's destiny in Christ for beloved community. One of Luther's earliest hymns, "Dear Christians, One and All Rejoice,"[9] recapitulates the entire canonical story from Genesis to Revelation. Dated to 1523, it provides a thematic overview of Luther's biblical theology in all its original freshness and rewards careful study.

In fact, this hymn has been the subject of considerable recent scholarly attention. Oswald Bayer lifts it up in his compelling re-presentation of Luther's theology in order to highlight the genuinely *miraculous* nature of God's mercy.[10] God's mercy, according to Bayer's interpretation of Luther, is not a given. It's not God's default position, so to speak, on which we can naturally count. It is extraordinary, for mercy costs God dearly. Calling to mind Hosea 11:8–9, Bayer sees mercy as an "overthrow [German *Umsturz*] in God himself." In his view, the fifth verse of our hymn, which has God the Father say "to His beloved Son: 'Tis time to have compassion," reflects this genuinely miraculous "overthrow," a spontaneous but costly turn in God from wrath to mercy expressed in the sending of the Son to bear away the sin of the world on the cross. This, then, would be the chief reference of the metaphor of Christ's death as a sacrifice of atonement: God causes God to surpass wrath and to create mercy in the cross and resurrection of Christ. This "overthrow" in God is what the Bible refers to in all its metaphorical speech concerning the coming of God to creatures.

In response to Bayer's impressive interpretation of the hymn, Christine Helmer seeks to recast Bayer's "overthrow" by pointing to God's boundless and eternal compassion and thus to avoid depicting

God, as Bayer's interpretation seems to allow, as an irrational bundle of contrary passions, the fury of wrath turning to mercy without any internal motivation.[11] For Helmer's interpretation of Luther, all God's ways are compassion, for God *is* love. Even the human experience of lostness is something reconstructed in hindsight from the new perspective of faith in God's compassion that comes through the gospel. Helmer accomplishes this shift from Bayer's reading by requiring greater attention to the genre of Luther's hymn as biblical "remembrance."

In the Bible, especially the Psalms, remembrance is not mere recollection of past facts as the way they really were but the active retrieval of the specific past of God's promise in order to ground present faithfulness; "remembrance" is the interpretive retrieval of the past into the present to fortify the besieged believer under trial to persevere till God's promised future arrives. Helmer thus urges that verses 2 and 3 of "Dear Christians, One and All Rejoice" (see appendix), which depict the previous state of believers as lost, helpless, and miserable puppets of sin under Satan's dominion, are not recalled as if they were reporting the previous self's state of consciousness—let alone God's wrathful state of consciousness! Rather, verses 2 and 3 are constructed as the present self's new interpretation of its former existence. This has the effect of recasting the tension between wrath and mercy, which for Bayer is a real tension resolved in God Himself. Since all God's ways are compassion, verses 2 and 3 represent the believer's retrospective self-interpretation of her previous misery in sin in ignorance of God's love. The believer so makes sense of the past from the perspective of her newfound awareness of God's boundless and eternal mercy.

The dispute between these two scholars surrounds the mysterious sudden plunge from the joyful call to rejoicing in verse 1 to the lament over human lostness in verses 2 and 3. For Bayer, this transition is and must be regarded as inexplicable fact, as inexplicable as the mystery of the origin of sin yet as real as God's wrath, which now falls upon that sin. For Helmer, Bayer's account of the transition from verse 1 to verse 2 not only is unintelligible as an interpretation of the hymn but also undermines the key theme of the eternal compassion of God.

But if we attend to verse 4, Luther describes God in eternity foreseeing that the cost of creation would be the cross of the incarnate Son. This glimpse of God's eternal self-determination to be the savior of sinners unites the concerns of both of these excellent Luther scholars. Boundless divine compassion from all eternity is indeed for Luther the divine motive and mode of operation in all God's ways. Thus for Luther, God undertakes creation with a view to redemption. As Luther put it in the Large Catechism, God has "created us for no other purpose than to redeem us." This is the proper meaning of "predestination"—not some predetermined list of the saved and the damned, but God's self-determination from the beginning to redeem and fulfill the creation through the missions of His Son and Spirit. The Son is the Lamb slain before the foundation of the world! The eternal counsel and purpose of God to love us accounts for what Bayer calls the "overthrow" in God—not as if it were a purely temporal reaction of God, being jerked around by conflicting emotions in reaction to human faith or faithlessness, but rather an eternally proactive decision to engage in the time of the creature, even making the sin and woe of the world His own and, in just this costly way, overcoming it. The divine transition from wrath to mercy takes place, not in the sense of a fit of passion, but as the passion of love achieving love for what is really against love by the costly way of the incarnation and cross of the Son. Building on the glimpse into the eternal counsel of the Trinity to save in verse 4, we can call this the event of "God surpassing God," love's overachievement, so to speak.

We may well wonder today whether this event of God surpassing God to find mercy in Christ for "real, not imaginary sinners," as Luther depicts in verses 2 and 3 of the hymn, is an answer to a question that no one is asking. Indeed, it is. For we modern people are not only epistemological foundationalists, but for similar reasons we are one and all "Pelagians"—those who think not only that we are saved by our "good works" but also that "good works" are achieved rather easily, almost naturally. This self-confident attitude is what Reinhold Niebuhr called the "easy conscience of modern man." We think that our goodwill may be taken for granted; that if we sin, it is mistake and error, not betrayal of our common humanity or offense against creation's Lord; and that if perchance we do sin seriously, we are not at personal fault since we are caught up in the causal nexus that forces us to act badly. Just as we can found knowledge in our personal experience or reflection, we can do good that makes us worthy of self-respect and the respect of others. The fact is that none of this procedure actually works anymore.

All the same, nothing more offends the easy conscience of the modern person than Luther's emphatic and more or less *catholic* teaching of original sin. Indeed, Luther criticized his contemporary Catholic opponents for being soft on original sin. They reduced original sin in the baptized to mere smoldering embers, identified as the bodily desire that could erupt into flames of lust. They did not, as a result, locate sinfulness in the highest human powers of will and reason, nor did they see it as an active rebel in the world that continues to penetrate the believer through her organic connection in the body to the unbelieving and rebellious world. As a result, for Luther contemporaneous "Catholics" did not take sin seriously enough!

Original sin—or rather, "inherited sin," as Luther preferred to put it, to lay the stress on our present state instead of Adam's original fault—means that we are caught up as heirs in a dysfunctional family legacy going back to Adam; as a result, we have before God only evil choices until God's choice in Jesus Christ takes hold of us. Only evil choices! Even our religious and ethical choices at their very best are evil choices. Luther got this from his study of Romans 2, where Paul the apostle speaks of the subtle sinfulness of good people, law-abiding people, excellent neighbors, and responsible citizens. As if that teaching were not severe enough, Luther goes on to say that we become personally responsible in these inevitably evil choices, which we make for our own part freely and joyfully. Luther not only takes up the doctrine of original sin from the Catholic tradition ("in sin my mother bore me," as verse 2 of "Dear Christians, One and All Rejoice" has us sing), but his apocalyptically radical appropriation of it makes the offense even worse—if that is possible! For Luther, as a result, any future "hell" pales in comparison to the present imprisoned and tortured state of the bound and deluded self, as verse 2 of the hymn depicts.

Let's clear up a roadblock to intelligibility here. Luther is speaking of *sin*, not *sins*—of the state of sinfulness, not transgressions. He is speaking of a spiritual power that captivates our desire. Such love, at the root of human being, rightly belongs to God above all and hence for all of God's creatures, our neighbors as for ourselves. Luther is not focusing on various transgressions of visible law, such as the political order is competent to see and judge. He is speaking not of human judgment but of God's judgment—not about externally keeping the law but about fulfilling it with free, joyful, and filial obedience.

This teaching on sin as a captivating power working death requires a basic distinction in perspectives under which we consider human responsibility, as Gerhard Ebeling taught us, between relations *coram Deo* (before God) and *coram hominibus* (before human beings) or *coram mundo* (before the world). To understand Luther's over-the-top discourse on sinfulness, one must always supply the implied relation: *coram Deo*, in relation to God. For example, if in my rage I draw the revolver to shoot my offending neighbor but the weapon malfunctions, the crime of murder (*coram mundo*) does not occur, even though the sin (*coram Deo*) surely does. Or again, if out of a desire to burnish my reputation for philanthropy I escort a senior citizen across a busy street, the good work for her benefit (*coram mundo*) occurs, but so the does the sin (*coram Deo*) of my prideful self-love. These illustrations illuminate the issue only partially, however, since they do not grasp the social nature of sinfulness.

One helpful contemporary way to explicate this distinction, then, is to point out how human judgment has an individualistic bias that ignores the social web in which the individual is entangled. I may be a courageous solider—serving in the Nazi *Wehrmacht*. I may be a conscientious taxpayer—funding the napalm bombing of villages in Vietnam "to save them." I may even heroically protest unjust wars—but fail to persuade others to cease and desist because I am unwilling to pay the personal price of genuine resistance by withholding taxes and going to prison as a conscientious objector to an immoral war. I may be a "moral man" in my personal existence, as Niebuhr explained the easy conscience of modern people, yet an unconscious but willing puppet of "immoral society." Original sin points to the overwhelming power of this trans-individual, social nexus of human sinfulness; we are born children of a fallen humanity. It is of course true that before our fellow human beings the individual choices we make in the world matter, even if at their best they are contaminated by sinfulness before God. Some evils are much less than others in society. As Hannah Arendt rightly pointed out in *Eichmann in Jerusalem*, if everyone is guilty, then no one is guilty. Recalling the example above of escorting a senior citizen: how much better for the world that I help the person through the dangerous traffic than to do nothing, paralyzed by scruples about my own mixed motives in helping! Or how important to judge the crimes of Eichmann rather than to excuse them!

As offensive as Luther's teaching on sin has been to modernity, it corresponds to more searching, contemporary postmodern sensibilities, traumatized as we are today by the failure of the great secular dreams of human emancipation that stemmed from the Enlightenment. These are the disasters of the twentieth century: Hitler, Hiroshima, and Stalin. Or think, as we do more and more nowadays, of the dark underside of American exceptionalism: the African slave trade, the Trail of Tears, and manifest destiny. As those of us in the United States now face the decline of our nation from its status as the world's sole superpower, and as our crippling debt and lack of social justice catch up with us, perhaps we can catch up with Luther. Against the overconfidence of the Enlightenment, Luther knew that human reason does not easily transcend particular interest but rather sells itself to the highest bidder. He foresaw our kind of greedy culture, where anything can be bought or sold—that is, where anything can be rationalized by the logic of the market, which is no longer confined to the market but is creeping into everything, even religion, which in America has become big business!

The Enlightenment critics of traditional European Christendom have every right to be critical, but, as Karl Barth often remarked, they are not critical enough to see our modern corruption and its deliverances in Verdun and Stalingrad, Auschwitz and the Killing Fields, terrorism and counterterrorism—to see all these as the wrath of God delivering the consequences of our greed and envy back upon us. When we turn to the personal side of contemporary life, the restoration of the "innocence of becoming" that Rousseau and Nietzsche dreamed of seems ever more distant in this tawdry culture of pornographic violence that saturates us. In this perspective, verses 2 and 3 of "Dear Christians, One and All Rejoice" are indeed a veritable revelation of what is *really* going on.

One of Luther's great discoveries, which made such penetrating prophecy possible, was how the Platonic tradition with its rationalistic optimism misinterpreted Paul's teaching on the conflict between the Spirit and the flesh (see, e.g., Gal. 5:16–26). Platonism cast the human moral conflict *repressively*—that is, as a battle of the mind for supremacy over wayward bodily desires. Overly optimistic in regard to the power of disinterested and innocent reason, and overly puritanical in regard to bodily desire, Platonism blamed the powerful evil body for subverting the weaker but innocent rational soul. But following Augustine, Luther interpreted Paul as meaning that humans sin by virtue of their highest powers, the very ones that distinguish us from the animals—namely, will and reason. We *want* to be god without God, and, acting *deliberately* on this spiritual desire by the *cunning* imaginations of our minds, we live "according to the flesh"—that is, according to human brainpower or muscle power, or both. Nowadays we think that technology is going to save us, as if lack of power, not of love and wisdom and justice, were the root of our problems. "Spirit," by contrast with reliance on the flesh, is not the human mind: mind over matter, intelligence over brute force. It is not intelligence, which can intelligently design the death factory at Auschwitz just as well as new therapies for treatment of cancer. It is the Spirit—of the Father and the Son! This *Holy* Spirit comes upon us from outside the self as the power and personal resolve to rely "in the flesh" on God's promise to be our God; the Spirit is the One who led Jesus to Gethsemane and who leads believers to their own new lives of resistance by working the Gethsemane of their own souls.

Thus Luther takes a jaundiced view of our vaunted "free will"—precisely in order, as we shall see in the next chapter, to hold fast to the freedom for which Christ has set us free (Gal. 5:1). For him, "free will" amounts to little more than consumer choice in a Walmart filled with inferior goods—the manipulation of bad choices. Before God such choices don't matter when the whole market is rigged by Satan's manipulation. Thus Luther contrasts the futile choices of "free will" with God's costly choice in all eternity: "Then God beheld my wretched state / With deep commiseration." Verse 4 of the hymn introduces the new view of predestination, as mentioned above: God's eternal choice or self-determination at the great cost of the Son's incarnate life and death on the cross to redeem and to heal the lost creature. From this grounding in God's eternal self-determination, all the other great narrative themes of Luther's Reformation theology unfold in due course of the hymn: (1) trinitarian advent (vv. 5–6, and again in 9)—that is, that God's coming is the inclusion of the creature in the Trinity's own eternal life; and (2) the mighty duel (v. 6) and joyful exchange (vv. 7–8)—that is, that by His incarnation, Christ triumphed over the devil not merely by power but also by right so that by His Word and Spirit, Christ is present in faith to unite with believers ("I am yours and you are mine") in the specific way of exchanging His innocence for the believer's sin. More on these themes in chapters 3 and 4.

By the time Luther composed this hymn, however, the early joy of the Reformation theology was already tempered by the outbreak of "other spirits" than the Holy Spirit of the Father and the Son. Thus the hymn ends with a warning from the lips of Christ: "Take heed lest men with base alloy / The heavenly treasure should destroy." That "base alloy" comes from the confusion of the Holy Spirit with inner voices, personal fantasies, or religious experiences or imaginations. But *this* figure of the biblical narrative, as we have seen, drives out the unholy spirits as He drives Jesus to His messianic ministry and destiny; *this* is the *Holy* Spirit, the Spirit *of the Father and the Son*, an identifiable *person*, not an impersonal power or energy. Luther named this dangerous confusion of the Holy Spirit with our own inner energies "enthusiasm"—literally, presuming to possess God, as if one had swallowed the Holy Spirit, as Luther joked in reference to the dove at Jesus's baptism, "feathers and all." Rather, the Holy Spirit has us when, by the external word of the Scriptures, we are driven to conformity to the eternal Word made flesh for us and for our salvation.

3

Evangelization

Secular Humanism and Christian Mission

One way to understand "secular humanism," which became the faith of the elite in European and American civilization in the last centuries, is as a kind of perverse fulfillment of Luther's Reformation turn to the secular as the site of sanctification. But this interpretation would indeed be perverse. Brad S. Gregory's *The Unintended Reformation* therefore underscores that this fulfillment was far from what Luther intended and is in fact more the consequence of the untenable treatment by all the dissenting protestors (i.e., the Protestants) of the Bible as self-interpreting. They were agreed in protesting the claim of Rome to monopolize the interpretation of the Bible, but when they turned to the Bible for its clear meaning, chaos broke out and turned, in time, into religious violence. Secular humanism arose precisely as an alternative to this chaos of Protestant Bible interpretation and the endless fighting it generated.

The philosophers Thomas Hobbes and Baruch Spinoza each in his own way tried to root out this "superstition," or "enthusiasm" (literally, being "possessed by a deity"), as they termed it. They put the crosshairs squarely on Paul's distinction between Adam and Christ, or Augustine's distinction between the earthly city and the city of God, or Luther's distinction between the reign of the devil and the reign of God. In some contrast to Augustine, but arguably closer to Paul, Luther drew the distinction between the contending reigns of God and the devil through *all* institutions, including church and state, rather than merely between church and state. Be that as it may, *any* such distinctions were anathema to the modern thinkers of secularism. There is only *one* world, *this* world as *known by human reason,* hence "secular humanism." But why should human reason now assume this sovereign and virtually divine status formerly occupied by God? How is it possible that human reason had erred formerly in superstition and enthusiasm but now could safeguard against a fall into error?

René Descartes transformed the former distinction between Creator and creature into a new distinction between thinking things and extended things, two realms inner and outer to the human self. This distinction satisfied his demand for clear and certain ideas that could serve as the foundation for knowledge. The demand for such clarity as could provide certainty was radical, and Descartes pursued this by doubting all candidates until bedrock certainty could be established. Thus outward appearances of sense were disqualified as shifting and momentary. Inward experiences could be illusions or hallucinations. Finally, Descartes came to the one certainty of a finite thinking thing: I cannot doubt that I doubt. From this certainty he deduced the famous conclusion "I think, therefore I exist." That is something, not nothing, in the search for a new foundation of knowledge that is not God, who is the author of both mind and matter. Yet Descartes's modern self exists as a thinking thing liable to misperception and illusion by its own embodiment! How will the finite thinking thing ever gain mastery over the external world, beginning with its own body?

To accomplish this task of human mastery, Descartes repurposed God as the metaphysical bridge between the thinking thing (the calculating and sovereign mind of modernity) and physical things out there in space (the physical environment); thus God exists to guarantee the human mind's access to and domination over the physical world. This was the decisive move in the origins of "secular humanism."

Empiricists, beginning with Locke, merely argued that the foundation of certainty was in fact sense perception. This was but a rival foundationalism, not a genuine alternative to it. Kant, who synthesized Descartes and Locke when provoked by the rather more consistent skepticism of Hume, in the end allowed the modern idea of God only as a permissible hope for those living according to reason in a world where raw force still seemed to reign. After Kant the German idealists, who in the second generation with Feuerbach and Marx became materialists, were bolder. Their basic thought was that the idea of an otherworldly God had died in the progress of civilization so that the now-dead idea of God was being resurrected into the human vocation to rule the earth as God was supposed to have done in previous, less enlightened ages. In all this, the new "gospel" of liberated and liberating humanity summoned up an activation of humanity to cast off immaturity, to rise up to free critical thinking, and to take care of the well-being of the human race by forcing nature to serve human interests.

This "secular humanism" has been the bogeyman of the evangelical imagination, especially during the twentieth century; but truth be told, evangelicalism has shared in the activist temperament from the time of its own origins during the rise of modernity. Whether in abolitionism or prohibitionism, in crusader wars to end all wars, or in the evangelization of the world in the "Christian century," evangelicalism's own version of secular humanism consisted in "can do" optimism that the globe could be conquered for Christ—howsoever that conquest was conceived. Luther, as we shall see in this chapter, requires a serious qualification to this activism. But it is a qualification that also grounds Christian mission in a better way.

More recently—after Hitler, Stalin, and Hiroshima—a darker vision has taken hold of the secular humanists. After Hitler, they increasingly saw that Darwin's idea is indeed ethically dangerous; after Hiroshima, that technology is not a mere servant of human masters but takes on an ominous life of its own; and after Stalin, that science and state can be bought and sold such that Marxism is not an alternative to capitalism but is itself an exponent of its all-encompassing grip. In sum, *moral* progress is *not* baked into the juggernaut of history. Domination over nature is no panacea; rather, insofar as human beings remain natural beings, they themselves become dominated by the means of "biopolitical" domination. This darker vision of contemporary thinkers like Giorgio Agamben exposes us "secular humanists" as helpless to stop "progress," even though for any with eyes to see, the unsustainable juggernaut unleashed in modernity portends ecological and/or economic collapse.

At root, this widespread current disillusionment (sometimes this is what is meant by "postmodernism" or "post-humanism") amounts to a "decentering" of the modern self as imagined by Descartes, Kant, and the idealists and materialists of the nineteenth century, who had presumed upon the coming humanity's sovereign status and quasi-divine vocation. Disillusionment follows on an exposé showing that in our own actions we are servants, not lords, agents as patients, doers as receivers. Activism blind to its own pathos does not liberate but rather exacerbates such bondage because it systematically blinds us to the powers that in fact hold us in thrall. In that case, the real issue now and for the future is not whether we have a lord but what lord we have.

And that is where a fresh encounter with Luther might help evangelicalism today learn to sharply distinguish between proselytism and evangelism. When Luther teaches Christians to confess that they cannot come to their Lord Jesus Christ by their own reason or effort, but rather have been called by the Spirit through the gospel into the *ecclesia*, he takes the "success" of proclamation and witness out of the hands of Christians. He puts Christians in mission at the mercy of the Spirit so that, like Paul the apostle, they must renounce shameful things, refuse to practice cunning or to falsify God's word, and instead commend the ministry of the gospel to the conscience of all people "by the open statement of the truth" (2 Cor. 4:2).

The Freedom of a Christian

In *The Freedom of a Christian* (1520),[1] the still-not-excommunicated Luther prefaces an open letter to Pope Leo X by expounding his teaching on the believer's paradoxical existence as king in Christ yet, just so, priestly servant to all—thus a "little Christ," or in plain language a "Christian" in deed to the neighbor. The charm of this treatise is that in it Luther sets forth his theology in a series of engaging images and motifs without the polemical vitriol that characterizes his writings after his excommunication. Some time later he drew the dire conclusion that if the pope in Rome had condemned his theology, manifestly drawn from Paul and Augustine, the papacy had condemned Christian doctrine itself and must be the long-prophesied antichrist taking its seat in the temple of God according to 2 Thessalonians. From this Luther, unhappily, further concluded that one must fight fire with fire: verbal violence was permitted in apocalyptic warfare, following the examples of the Lord (Matt. 23; John 8:39–47) and of his apostle (Phil. 3:2). Neither conclusion served Luther, or Luther's theology, well in the future, though it was standard fare in its own day. Luther's resort to verbal violence, which he actually justified as the Christian alternative to physical violence, certainly stands today as an obstacle to our appropriation of him as a teacher of the ecumenical church. Thankfully, then, this programmatic treatise on Christian freedom comes from a time before the turn to the rhetorical violence of apocalyptic warfare was stamped into his writings.

Yet, as mentioned above regarding Hobbes and Spinoza, Luther's contrast between the "inner" and "outer" human being can be another kind of obstacle to our understanding. Even though it is drawn from the apostle Paul's usage (e.g., 2 Cor. 4:16), this contrast raises the eyebrows, especially of feminist theologians today, who are (rightly) suspicious of "anthropological dualisms"—that is, thought patterns that divide human beings into superior and inferior parts, such as brains and brawn, mind and body, private and public. They are rightly suspicious of such dualistic patterns of thought, because the sexual difference of male and female gets mapped according to such patterns into gender stereotypes, specifically inferiorizing women as body, emotion, and property in contrast to men as mind, logic, and owner. But is this what Luther, or Paul, meant by distinguishing the inner and the outer human being?

It would be anachronistic to call Luther a feminist, but in some respects he was a feminist before his time. The predominant form of feminism in America today is ideologically "liberal," in the sense that it aspires to maximize personal freedom or autonomy and equalize economic opportunity. When measured by this standard, Luther's historic affirmation in his own time of the woman in partnership with the man in marriage and household economy seems to lock women in the kitchen. But this measurement is anachronistic so far as it overlooks the massive economic changes since the nineteenth century that privatized the home as a haven in the heartless world of industrialism and wage labor. Consequently, it overlooks Luther's far more important and radical assaults on misogyny and the so-called double standard, which required women to be treated by men as either virgins or whores.

Luther struggled against questions of anthropological dualism in the direction of a holistic account of the human person moved by desires befitting a creature who does not have life in itself but must find its resources. Anthropological dualism had entered into the Christian theological tradition from Platonism or, more extremely, from gnosticism, as if to say that the mind or the inner self is kindred to God while the body or the mental-social self is a prison house or illusion of false consciousness inspired by the devil. Surely one of Luther's greatest achievements as a student of Paul was to discover that distinctions such as the inner and the outer person, or akin to it, spirit and flesh, are not *anthropological* dualisms at all. Rather, these oppositions signal the invasion of God's new creation coming to redeem the fallen world. They are reflections of the battle between the kingdom of God and the kingdom of the devil, the city of God and the earthly city, humanity in Christ and humanity in Adam.

The "inner man," then, is the freed prisoner, the liberated *person*, the *conscience* ransomed by Christ that struggles against the bondage of the outer person, who is the person's own *body* organically linked to the fallen world of malice and injustice. Thus the justified person struggles in the Spirit against the sinful flesh. The differentiation is not between parts of human beings that can be ranked as superior and inferior. The differentiation is between the liberated human being called by the gospel to trust in God and the same being still in bondage as a member, if not a subject, of the fallen world by virtue of its body that must eat and drink, labor and rest, obey or rebel in the world as yet unredeemed. Hence, Luther's treatise title accentuates the freedom of a Christian as one freed by Christ, capturing the Pauline indicative and imperative: "For freedom Christ has set us free. Stand firm, therefore, and do not submit again to a yoke of slavery" (Gal. 5:1). This freedom is precisely not "an opportunity for self-indulgence, but through love [to] become slaves to one another" (5:13). While the outer man still remains in bondage to the dying world, the inner man has now been freed. Christians live in this tension between the already of freedom and the not yet of bondage. One would have to be in heaven, for Luther, with a new spiritual body solely and radiantly resourced by the light of God's glory, for it to be otherwise.

Luther sets forth the proper understanding of this apocalyptic, not anthropological, dualism with the famous paradox "A Christian is a perfectly free lord of all, subject to none. A Christian is a perfectly dutiful servant of all, subject to all." A paradox, as we previously heard, is a rhetorical device that asserts an apparent contradiction. An apparent contradiction either proves to be nonsense—that is, nothing but a contradiction—or it yields a new and unanticipated meaning that has never before existed in the world, for which, then, there has been no readily available language. The latter is Luther's intention with paradox: true freedom is not, as people ordinarily think, getting to do whatever one wants; rather, it is being set free to love and serve.

This is the new meaning of the true humanity that has come into the world in Jesus Christ. Jesus Christ is the One who was free to love and indeed freely loved us who were not worthy of love but rather worthy of the holy judgment that falls on what is not loving. And because the Christian is first of all (and always first of all!) the one beloved in this way by Jesus Christ, the Christian lives in baptismal union with Him, dying to the former existence of Adam—curved into self as though the center of the universe—and now being raised to the new existence of a free and joyful obedience. This new obedience consists in ecstasy, which means, literally, to stand outside oneself.

Get the picture? The sinner, Adam, is curved into himself as though his belly were the center of the universe—the very "centered" self of modernity! The saint, in Christ, is curved out of self to trust in God and to love for the neighbor and to hope for the world. Just this, moreover, is what Luther meant by the certainty or assurance of faith, not introspection but, so to speak, extraspection. This ecstasy or rapture, as Luther sometimes put it, is the new life in Christ; the freedom of the Christian is being freed by Christ to live before God our heavenly Father as a "little" Christ to the neighbor—that is, like the One who served (Mark 10:45)—filling the image of God that she is by creation with the likeness to Jesus Christ by new creation.

As mentioned, Luther's treatise on Christian liberation is chock-full of charming and powerful images. Believers are "saturated and intoxicated" with the promises of God. Union with Christ is a "joyful exchange" of nuptials, sealed by the "wedding ring" of faith. The freed Christian engages in battle against sin, death, and the power of the devil under the rule of her Lord Jesus, who first and foremost fought a "mighty duel" with Satan. For the accuser arms himself with the accusing law of God in order to drive sinners to despair with the knowledge of their sin and in this way to bring them back into his bondage, as if they had not been ransomed and set free by Christ's priestly death and kingly resurrection.

Accompanying these powerful images of the historical event of the encounter of Christ and faith through the announcement of the gospel is an equally powerful concept for the enlightened (that is to say, theological) understanding, appropriation, and use of these images and motifs by preachers—namely, the proper distinction between God's Word at work as law and as gospel (or promise). This "proper" distinction is *not* a distinction between Jewish legalism and Christian permissiveness. It is *not* any kind of anthropological or religious distinction at all. It is a distinction that pertains to the one Word of God, who is Jesus Christ, the incarnate Son who fulfilled all righteousness for us. The message of the cross of the

Son of God can be, of course, terrifying, as the Gospel accounts of the cosmos darkening at the hour of His death attest. That is God's Word as law, demanding what is impossible from sinners who cannot fix themselves and thereby exposing a guilty human impotence. But this same Word of the incarnate Son, who died at our hands to expose our lovelessness, becomes good news for us as the same Son rises victorious, surpassing God's Word against us by his limitless solidarity of love for us, and so winning us to repentance and faith by the gift of His own Spirit.

The use of the verb "surpass" here does not suggest that either God's holy demand or human failure is an illusion or misunderstanding that may be easily set aside. It is God who demands righteousness of the creature by the law and judges whether anyone is a doer of the law, not a hearer only. This demand is no illusion. Rather, "surpass" means that in Christ, God has nevertheless sought and found the way to us, albeit under wrath because we were hearers only, not fulfillers of the law. "God surpassing God" is an expression that tries to capture the dynamic movement of God in coming to creatures lost to Him by sin and death. It grounds this movement in the eternal generation of the Son by the Father, since God is God who can and did so love the lost world that He gave His own Son. God the Father is eternally God surpassing God, and thus also in time is God whose heart recoils within Him, whose compassion grows warm and tender, and who is not an irate husband coming to destroy a faithless spouse—as Hosea preaches—but the Holy One in our midst, full of grace and truth. God surpassing God, then, is not the philosopher Hegel's kenotic collapse of God by a total self-emptying into humanity, which now rises up in place of the otherworldly God to take on his traditional role—the apotheosis of the sovereign self of modernity. God surpassing God is Luther's mighty duel and joyful exchange!

From this teaching of Paul, Luther draws the conclusion that the law informs but does not reform or empower the sinner actually to become righteous. Indeed it even works wrath by calling the bluff of the proud and confident, provoking the sinful self on to the sublime sin of self-justification, only finally to work despair by unveiling the futility of this very effort at self-justification that it has provoked. To this eventual despair of self in true repentance, as to the way prepared for the coming of the Lord, the promise of God now comes on the scene to give what the law sought—namely, a new heart to fulfill what the law required, giving faith from the heart, *ex corde*, in the God who surprisingly, amazingly justifies the ungodly.

Faith, which assents to the promise attending the news of Christ and entrusts the self to it, is the new obedience. Faith empowers the sinner to become righteous. Faith fulfills the law. For faith gives God His due, acknowledging God as the Giver of all gifts, and hence also gives the neighbor what is her due—namely, the love that is needed, urgently needed, here and now in this world. Faith is thus the true worship of God, and by the same token, at the root of all sin is nothing but unfaith.

Personal and Social Righteousness

Recall the distinction previously introduced between the perspectives *coram Deo* and *coram hominibus*. In the latter perspective any upright citizen *observes* the "works of the law" outwardly—think of a visible checklist of good deeds to be performed and evil deeds to be avoided like the Ten Commandments provide. In any functional society, there are relatively few transgressors in this perspective. This capacity to conform socially by outward observance of the law was tagged "civil righteousness" in the Reformation, the kind of righteousness that lawyers and philosophers understand and value. It marks the difference between civilized life and barbarism. That boundary is certainly not to be despised!

But the deeper truth seen in theological perspective is that civil righteousness is nothing more before God than enlightened self-interest—and so it can and does lead to entire societies or cultures having a smug sense of superiority over others, utterly blind to the way this sense of superiority perniciously inferiorizes others and even exploits them for its own enlightened purposes in this stigmatization. Think of the racist trope of colonialism about "little brown brothers whom we are teaching to make a living through an honest day's labor." This is a "systemic" racism that postcolonial inquiries are making plain again in our times.

For Luther, the old Adamic self, curved into itself, remains in power in civil righteousness, doing the good to avoid punishment and to gain status in a society where social sins go systematically unnoticed. This civic righteousness is not the love of God above all and of all creatures in and under God that flows from the heart, as Luther writes, which actively seeks to be neighbor to any wounded one on the road. Rather, it is the love for me and mine, which uses God and all others for its own good. But only faith alone in Christ alone brings free, creative, and joyful love. Such faith does not merely observe the external works of the law but rather fulfills the law's spiritual intention.

At the conclusion of the treatise on Christian freedom, Luther deals with certain objections that are still important to us today. Let us mention three. First, if Christians are freed by Christ to love, why does Luther insist that they are still sinners? One must not think here of transgressions such as can be known and identified readily by a list of prohibitions like the Ten Commandments provide, and thus judged by civil righteousness. One must think radically of sinfulness as bondage to godless self-concern in all things. Thus Luther answers the objection to his *simul iustus et peccator* by saying that Christians above all are those who know that the parousia has not yet come! The battle is but inaugurated in the coming of faith and thus still rages, not only around believers but also in them. They are not yet in heaven, not yet the glorified bodies of the new creation in its fullness and power. The righteousness of the Christian in conscience by faith exists simultaneously with the Christian's being a member, though not a subject, of the fallen and sinful creation. Luther takes the depiction of the divided self in Romans 7 (following the account of baptism into Christ's death in Rom. 6) as typifying the *Christian* experience: "I do not do the good I want, but the evil I do not want is what I do. . . . Who will rescue me from this body of death?" (vv. 19, 24). The answer to this lament, for Luther, is described in Romans 8 as nothing less than the reconciliation of the cosmos at the revelation of the glorious liberty of the children of God that brings about the redemption of our bodies at the resurrection.

In the interim, then, Christian growth in holiness consists in "mortification of the flesh"—not language we are likely to use today, but the concept here is crucial. One grows in Christian righteousness by not giving vent to the desires of the flesh (not, as we have heard, sexual desire but rather the mind's desire to be God and not let God be God). And the Christian grows in holiness by assenting to the reign of the Spirit, bearing fruits of love, joy, and peace. Christian life, for Luther, is a battle, a personal "jihad," as it were, putting to death the old self formed in Adam, giving way progressively to the new self formed in Christ. This battle rages today and tomorrow and only ends with the resurrection of the dead—not before!

A second objection questions whether Luther's Pauline account of sinfulness is so radical that it undercuts every effort to improve this world in the direction of civil righteousness or, as we say today, social justice. Luther answers quite clearly, "Our faith in Christ does not free us from works but from false opinions concerning works, that is, from the foolish presumption that justification is acquired by works. . . . [Thus] works of the body are not to be despised or neglected." The dispute, in other words, is not about whether Christians are to do good works but about what counts as a truly good work. Being a good soldier or citizen or club member or family member can all be in service of a sinful regime. Think of brave Nazis or loyal Soviets or engaged Ku Klux Klansmen or the Hatfields and the McCoys.

In the politics of a fallen creation, good works done for others are most often little more than civic righteousness. Luther's first and essential point about civic righteousness is that we should not have any messianic illusions about the goodness of such works, which will betray all the blind spots and self-satisfactions of any given society. Change we can believe in will come with the parousia of Christ. Until then, sober Christians who work while it is day do not despise the works of the body, including the work of social justice; but they free themselves and others from false opinions about what we are accomplishing, if indeed we accomplish anything truly good at all. Does this sound too meager to inspire social change? When one thinks of the string of unprecedented atrocities committed in the modern secular world in the name of social justice (Hitler, Hiroshima, and Stalin!), Luther's Christian realism about good works and social justice is a welcome and much-needed antidote to self-righteous zealotry, old and new.

I mention one more objection that Luther anticipates, really an original and deeply influential misunderstanding of the Christian freedom that he describes in this treatise. This is the view of the iconoclasts, the "image-smashers." Such "want to show that they are free men and Christians only by despising and finding fault with ceremonies, traditions, and human laws; as if they were Christians because on stated days they do not fast or eat meat when others fast." Sanctimonious abstention from religious works is, however, simply the same legalism inverted. It now procures righteousness by refraining from religious works and demanding that others also abstain. But no one becomes righteous by not observing them any more than by observing them! Paul teaches something far better: that "neither circumcision *nor uncircumcision* is anything; but a new creation is everything!" (Gal. 6:15, emphasis added). This is Paul's "canon," his rule of faith (*regula fidei*) that he teaches in all his churches (6:16). Luther sees this rule of true freedom as the freedom to love, and retrieves it. The freedom of a Christian is the battle to love in earnest a world still ruled by mendacity and malice—which are also found, if not preeminently, in the religion business itself.

Thus, society is capable of reform and moral progress; this becomes possible in society precisely when, knowing the limits of human power, we do what is within our power and let God be God to do what is not in our power or competence. Luther rejects the path of revolutionary violence, but this does not mean that he abandons the reform of society. Because he thinks the creation of God is good, moreover, he does not believe that social reform consists in any kind of violent remaking of things. Reform is rather a matter of what love in its creative imagination discovers in the practical tasks of social life. These arenas are, for Luther, the domestic economy, organized religion, and political governance. Luther finds all of these basic social institutions in the great text of Genesis 1:26–28, the "mandates" of creation, as Dietrich Bonhoeffer called them.

Vocation and Perseverance

So Luther the theologian does not have a systematic program for social reform as such, but as a preacher in his own time and place he is willing to make critiques and propose alternatives. The policy details he leaves to practitioners, pastorally advising them that God is pleased with such holy secularity and gives them heart and mind to make and keep human life human. The deep reason that Luther can leave reform in the hands of the baptized practitioners in society and not claim it for those ordained to serve Word and sacraments is that Luther believes that God's creation is continuous. No theologian attending to the Word can possibly have the acute awareness and experiential wisdom of the world in its development requisite to the reforms needed in the various arenas of social life.

What rather more concerns Luther is whether we will persevere in our vocations. The personal witness to Jesus Christ in the world lies with the baptized who persevere in their vocations. Here the witness is made not only with words but also in deeds in which the Word is incarnated as "little Christs" serve their neighbors. Here the Spirit finds occasion to draw others to the community of faith, where the gospel may be preached to evoke new faith and obedience in new people. Evangelism as a new-member campaign would be disincarnate proselytizing otherwise.

Luther is rightly concerned about perseverance because the vocation of holy secularity is tested sorely and daily. It is just here that questions of theodicy—of the justice of God in governing humanity—arise with great force, and it is the answer of tested and afflicted faith that bears witness in word and in deed to the gospel. If action and agency for Christians are the product of faith that receives righteousness and lives in the "hope of righteousness" (Gal. 5:5), hope is often dimmed by the cruel experience of the world's preference for the lie and hostility to what is right. How, then, does Christian agency persevere? What kind of theodicy does Luther provide for those anguished at the world's cruelty and indifference to truth? In point of spiritual fact, no question is more central today to speaking the good news in a world that is still in tears over unjust suffering at the hands of the malice of indifference.

God is incomparable. That means that there is none like God; it further means that God eternally is and remains beyond the comprehension of the creature. "Comprehension" in this context means to see and grasp from every possible angle so as to be able to control, manipulate, and predict a phenomenon. To say that God is incomprehensible, or "inscrutable," as Paul puts it in Romans 11:33, is to say something that applies in principle only to the one true God. The flip side of that acknowledgment, then, is that everything else in the world is in principle comprehensible—a matter of progressive scientific comprehension. This theological conviction thus lent support to the rise of the modern scientific worldview, particularly on the soil of the Lutheran reformation. It led to the great expansion of education, research, inquiry, and probing philosophical reflection seeking better and better accounts of human experience. Luther's reformatory "social gospel" consisted perhaps above all in this new impetus given to the God-given possibilities of knowledge of the world serving its humanization.

Interestingly, this double-sided conviction about God the Creator's incomparability and the comprehensibility of the creation is something that creatures come in faith to understand. "Understanding," in this connection, is not the kind of knowledge we have in scientific comprehension of phenomena but the capacity to recognize and identify a phenomenon sufficiently well to work practically with it. This pragmatic acknowledgment of God's uniqueness, or the incomparability that makes God incomprehensible theoretically but nonetheless followable and understandable practically, is not the product of philosophical reflection; it is the gift given with God's self-donation and self-communication in the gospel. "No one has ever seen God. It is God the only Son, who is close to the Father's heart, who has made him known" (John 1:18). This is the grace and truth that lightens our darkness. Luther knowingly termed this knowledge "the light of grace" in contrast to the darkness cloaking God's will and purpose in the mere "light of nature."

Thus, we understand and trust so that we can follow; we do not comprehend in a way that removes the need for trust now or for wonder eternally. Even in the light of glory, when faith will give way to sight and we will know even as we have been known, we will never comprehend God. Rather, God will be eternally fascinating, a mystery never to be fully plumbed. But we can already now in faith understand and follow on our sojourn through the lights of nature, grace, and glory.

Nature, Grace, and Glory

With these distinctions between various lights, Luther asks and answers the burning questions of theodicy concerning the justice of God in a world where he frankly and forcefully acknowledges that the wicked prosper and the righteous suffer. Luther does this at the conclusion of the brilliant but vexing treatise *The Bondage of the Will*. He exclaims, "To think that we cannot for a little while *believe* that He is just, when He has actually promised us that when He reveals His glory we shall clearly *see* that He both was and is just!"[2] Luther does not disregard the question of theodicy; rather, he disputes the possibility of a rational or philosophical theodicy by the light of nature. He acknowledges, moreover, that the light of grace does not resolve but amplifies the difficulty, since it is inexplicable how God "crowns the ungodly freely, without merit, and does not crown, but damns another."[3] Still, he does not disown the question of God "most righteous and evident," but refers to God in the light of glory. Luther knows his Old Testament all too well to abandon the question of theodicy as futile. He knows that the question about God's justice (that is, about the apparent lack of God's justice in our experience of this fallen and groaning world) rages like a devouring fire in the hearts of believers who doubt, as also in skeptics who would like to believe but cannot. But Luther does think that the only adequate theodicy, as God spoke to Job out of the whirlwind, is the one that God will provide on His great and glorious day when He reveals His justice. Then, with Israel, "we shall know that He is the Lord."

In the meantime, we have to focus the question in terms of the uniqueness of God, who is not like anything else in all His creation. Modern scholarship has taught us that the Shema, "Hear, O Israel: YHWH our God, YHWH *alone*!" (*not* the older translation, "YHWH is *one*"), is best understood as a henotheistic—not monotheistic—confession. Henotheism (adherence to one God) means that in a world awash with gods, idols, and demonic powers claiming authority and saving power, Israel is wed to YHWH alone, who brought Israel up out of the land of Egypt, the house of bondage. The sense of the claim, then, is that only YHWH saves in the way of the exodus, so that adherence to other gods will lead back into bondage.

Only later in Israel's journey with God—in the trauma of the exile, when Israel learned that she depended on YHWH to exist, not YHWH on her—did henotheism from the exodus mature into an articulate postexilic monotheism, that is, into the belief that there is only one true God, that other so-called gods are imposters. As we see in the preaching of Second Isaiah (Isa. 40–55), for example, YHWH claims this title of the one true God, the Creator of all that is not God. God is the God who is, strictly speaking, incomparable, not part of the created world but rather its Creator, not then like anything we know in the world, truly a God who hides Himself as clothed in the vast world He has made.

Luther the Old Testament scholar grasped these things. The incomparable one true God is inaccessible and incomprehensible to the light of nature, for we can by nature understand only what is similar to what we already know within the cosmos: other creatures like ourselves coming into being and passing away again. Here we naturally reason by analogies and similitudes, going from the greater known to the lesser known; for example, think of an American returning from the United Kingdom and explaining to another American, "Cricket is like baseball."

Now, Luther argues in the conclusion of *The Bondage of the Will* that if we think in this accustomed, natural way strictly on the basis of the evidence of creaturely experience, we are driven by the light of nature, if not to silence before the daunting question mark of God, then to blasphemy or atheism. For by the light of nature, and without blinders or illusions or mystifications, it seems that the one true God works all in all without discrimination, like the dharma of the Buddhists or the two-faced Shiva of the Hindus, both killing and making alive without any apparent order of justice or purpose in mind. If we take it personally, in the light of nature God seems like a malicious devil. If we take it impersonally as luck or chance, we can perhaps handle adversities with greater tranquility, but we are condemned to live out our lucky or unlucky lives in an objectively hopeless cosmos, humanly speaking. If we take it as dharma, on the other hand, we are condemned to expend great effort to liberate ourselves from the cycle of endlessly repeated sufferings. All this "light of nature," which is darkness concerning God, Luther packs into a few terse words!

The monotheistic claim to truth—that it is the saving LORD of the exodus who is the one true God—comes as a light shining in this darkness concerning God, as a *promise* to be held and trusted in faith by the light of grace, patiently awaiting its confirmation in the light of glory. It is the claim that at last the glory of the LORD shall be revealed, that YHWH who liberates the oppressed will prove to be the one true God.

This promise of the reign of God was the substance of Jesus's preaching concerning the coming kingdom of God and His own messianic claim to have already inaugurated its reality in those glorious moments of epiphany: the forgiveness of sins, the healing of the sick, the liberation of the possessed, and the raising of the dead. In Jesus we are given a glimpse of the light of glory, summed up in the transfiguration story. This glimpse of future glory now is what Luther calls the light of grace. If the light of nature had cast doubt on whether God cares for us, the light of grace demonstrates God's care in Easter and the exodus, just as these narrative promises point us forward to glory as the confirmation of this divine care for us. Hence Luther's potent conclusion, following Paul in Romans 8: "*There is a life after this life; and all that is not punished and repaid here will be punished and repaid there; for this life is nothing more than a precursor, or, rather, a beginning, of the life that is to come.*"

The motif of punishment, let us note in passing, is central to Luther's biblical theology. The scoundrels who have usurped the earth with malice and injustice will not forever get away with murder. The righteous who live by faith active in love and hope for the groaning earth will in turn be vindicated. The mature Luther does not reject the theology of glory, then, but rather sees that this glory remains future and is only paradoxically (*sub contrario*, under the opposite appearance) present to us now as a promise attested by Christ's Easter vindication—as a glimpse, a sign, for seeing, as in a mirror, enigmatically.

We need to stress what is technically called *inaugurated* eschatology—that in Christ's death and resurrection God inaugurates the coming glory so that believers baptized in Christ live in the creative tension between the already of their justification by faith and the not yet of their final vindication in the sight of all. Luther matured to the stance that God indeed kills—that is the theology of the cross, the "punishment" of sin—but *in order to* make alive, to give hope of glory, that the baptized might already now walk in newness of life. Unless this *purpose clause* prevails victoriously in our preaching and theology, giving us a glimpse of the glory to be revealed that is not worthy to be compared to the sufferings of this present age, the theology of the cross works nothing but despair and death. If that is all that it does, it is the work of the devil, not of God.

In this light, the problem of the theology of glory is not its promise of health, healing, prosperity, and wholeness but only that it imagines that we are already in heaven, that we have already arrived, that we have nothing further to expect from our saving Lord. But the risen Christ must reign until he subdues all enemies under his feet. And the last enemy to be destroyed is death. So the Easter preacher following Luther will so proclaim the light of grace that living now in hope for the light of glory becomes liberating newness of life amid sorrows and tears, that believers may persevere in the active Christian life.

Now, what about the difference between proselytism and evangelism? What about mission to the nations and pioneer proclamation that brings new people into the faith of the church? Does Luther collapse mission into vocation and holy secularity? Does this church in any active way call people in Jesus's name to repentance and faith?

We cannot help but observe that Luther at first has a sobering and even discouraging word about this that anticipates some critiques of the missionary movement of the evangelical expansion of the last two centuries. He asks searchingly whether we are expanding our own kingdoms or the kingdom of God, whether we are in the religion business or the kingdom business, whether we are manipulating emotions and surreptitiously appealing to human powers or leaving it to the Spirit to use the proclamation of the gospel to create faith where and when it pleases God. Historically, Luther became convinced that the world was about to end with the parousia of Christ amid the ravaging last battles—not a scenario that inspires new missionary activity. Nonetheless, he did envision what historian Scott Hendrix has called "recultivating the vineyard." To this end, he adopted and adapted the early church's catechetical method of teaching and instilling the faith of the gospel. We will take a thorough look at this way of evangelism in the final chapters of part 2, which analyze Luther's Large Catechism since it notes a form of evangelism other than the revivalist methodologies of evangelicalism, which likewise were seeking to reinvigorate moribund Christianity.

4

The Atonement

Meditation on Christ's Passion

In his early *Meditation on Christ's Passion* (1519),[1] Luther explains how to meditate fruitfully during Holy Week: not by scapegoating Jews or by trying to bribe God with self-flagellation or by sentimentality, but by realizing the cost of grace in the incarnate Son's suffering for me, the sinner, that I might be freed from the guilt burden of sin that weighs me down and rise up to begin to vanquish sin by following my saving Lord, who stoops to me through the cross to lift me to the crown. The point of departure is the apostolic command "Let the same mind be in you that was in Christ Jesus" (Phil. 2:5), and again, "Since therefore Christ suffered in the flesh, arm yourselves also with the same intention" (1 Pet. 4:1).

The command to meditate on Christ's passion points to an imitation of Christ, yet an imitation of His *mind*, His *intention*, not a mindless repetition of His recorded deeds, let alone a presumptuous imitation of the messianic work that is His alone. One could literally make a cord of whips and invade the local synagogue, but that would be anything but a true imitation of Christ, who drove the money changers out of the Father's house of prayer for all peoples. A true imitation of Christ's mind would be a similarly prophetic break with the religion business (scapegoating, bribing God, emotional manipulation in order to tyrannize consciences) in exchange for organizing ministry in the kingdom business of gathering all nations to the praise of God.

The truth is that the only way to follow Jesus literally would be to enter some kind of science-fiction time machine and find Him on the dusty byways of first-century Galilee, with His face set to go up to Jerusalem (Luke 9:51). Copying Christ's deeds is simply not possible, because the settings of His actions and ours are always historically different, making the actions undertaken in them unrepeatable with respect to their significance. But with the "mind of Christ"—we should always recall that Christ is the One anointed in the Spirit to do the saving works of Israel's true and promised son of David (Luke 4:18–19)—one moves the congregation away from the religion business into the kingdom business today with deeds not yet imagined in the New Testament, like sacrificially opening a day care center, or a homeless shelter, or a community garden, or equipping lay home visitors to call the lapsed to repentance and faith, and so on.

The *imitatio mentis* (imitation of the mind) is what is commanded of disciples who would follow Jesus through the cross to the crown. Being grounded in the mind of Christ, who suffered in the flesh, disciples with Christ-liberated minds can suffer and act in ever fresh and pertinent ways that advance the redemption and fulfillment of the suffering creation.

Luther diagnoses three mistaken ways of woodenly imitating deeds rather than the mind and motive revealed in Christ's deeds and sufferings. These are scapegoating, turning the cross into a talisman, and the demagogic cultivation of sentiment. Since the aged Luther sinned grievously in scapegoating Jews, here in this early work his insightful critique of popular preachers who whip up anti-Judaism in the name of meditating on the Lord's passion is particularly striking and important for us today. As a result, we can with justice pit Luther against Luther and understand precisely how the old man violated his own better insight.

As we shall shortly see, true meditation on Christ's passion brings to bear the divine judgment of the cross upon one who meditates—not any other. The late Gerhard Forde honed in on Luther's second line of criticism of those who turn the cross into an ornament—that is, "put roses on the cross" to make of it a good luck charm or a talisman with which to ward off Dracula or other such foolishness.[2] There is nothing magical, as we shall see, about the atonement. The one who meditates on the holy passion is crucified—not literally but spiritually, in the mind, in one's intentionality—with Christ, or the meditation is vain and the power claimed for it is an infantile indulgence in magical thinking. Perhaps Luther's critique of sentimentalism hits closest to home for us today, since the manipulation of emotion is the readiest and most widespread trick of the religion business. Preachers who never meditate at all on Christ's holy passion, let alone preach it regularly as the life-changing sacrifice of God for us in the apocalyptic drama of creation's redemption, can bring out the violins when it is time to drum up increased financial support: "He died for you. What will you give for Him?" *Ugh!*

It is important to notice that in this text Luther urges us to meditate on Christ's passion not as those who have never heard the gospel, nor as those who do not know of the resurrection, nor as persons needing to be convinced of and convicted to faith. It is as believers entering Holy Week that we meditate on Christ's passion to ground us, to deepen us, and to progress in faith operative in love and hope. Indeed, only those who believe, who already know the resurrection of the Crucified One, who thus live under grace and trust in the finality of God's mercy can enter into this darkest of places that they may further die to sin and rise to righteousness by the ongoing re-formation of their minds, reorganization of their affects, and presentation of their bodies for service (cf. Rom. 12:1–2). Luther thus begins the meditation with the "penal suffering" of Christ—that is, the biblical motif that tells how He who knew no sin was made to be sin (2 Cor. 5:21), how He who hung on the tree became "a curse for us" (Gal. 3:13) in order to be the "ransom for many" (Mark 10:45).

For a few good reasons but also for some very bad ones, much contemporary theology is repelled by this eminently biblical notion that Christ suffered the wrath of God in drinking the bitter cup on behalf of others. But, as Bonhoeffer famously observed, apart from the penal suffering of Christ in the place of the sinner as the basis of our free justification, we can hardly avoid the heresy of cheap grace. Cheap grace, Bonhoeffer wrote, turns grace into an idea (even a good idea, like hospitality) or a principle (like the good principle of inclusiveness) rather than the historical accomplishment of the obedient Christ, who suffered in the flesh for sinners and so also by His Spirit just as historically convinces and convicts anyone to faith in just this stumbling block, Christ crucified for our sins, proclaimed in our place. Because Christ bore our sins before God, His grace takes form in the world as the believer's mortification of the flesh and lifelong repentance as self-denying, cross-bearing discipleship that follows Jesus (spiritually, in the mind, in our intentionality). As Luther argued in the Ninety-Five Theses, purgatory is not future. Purgatory is now!

Surely Luther hit the nail on the head, then, when he identified the deep source of our contemporary repugnance at the thought of Christ innocently suffering the holy judgment of God on human sinfulness. If that be so, it terrifies! If that be so, "You are the man!" (2 Sam. 12:7)—*you* are the executioner of Him who suffers for you! Hell is not only or even chiefly some future threat but this present existential moment of meditation on the One who suffered and died, not in someone else's place, but in *your* place, the place of His *executioner*! Not, that means, by replacing you, but *in the very place that is your own, the place of the enemy of God.*

For Luther, Christ is not a literal sacrifice of atonement but rather a metaphorical one. Calling Luther's doctrine of the sacrifice of atonement "metaphorical," however, could be misleading; it might seem that Luther is saying that Jesus's death only symbolizes reconciliation rather than accomplishes it. But Luther is looking at the etymology of the word of Greek origin, *meta-phora*, which means an exchange or transfer. Its Latin equivalent is *trans-latio*, which likewise means an exchange or transfer. Applied to certain kinds of figurative language, metaphor indicates a transfer of meaning, like when I say, "My friend is a peach." What I mean by this exchange of meanings is not that my friend is hanging on a tree, ripe, plumb, and ready to pick, but that my friend is sweet (another metaphor!) to me.

So also when we say that Christ is a sacrifice of atonement, we do not mean that Christ is literally the scapegoat on whom our punishment is laid so that God's wrath is satisfied on it instead of us. For even that great sacrifice would leave us still in our sins, ever in need of further sacrifices (or reapplications of Christ's infinitely valuable sacrifice) to keep divine punishment at bay. Such was in fact one line of medieval thinking behind the repeated sacrifice of the Mass. But the exchange that took place on Calvary, Luther explains, is an exchange of meaning—and a *joyful* one at that. When we say that Christ is a sacrifice of atonement, we mean that Christ's death tells of a hitherto unheard-of priest who gives and offers not a scapegoat in place of sinners' punishment but Himself in loving solidarity with sinners. Astonishingly, He gives Himself into this solidarity of love all the way down to the grave and hell. Of course, that is not the end of the story, neither for Christ nor for the believer in Christ. Rather, on account of this solidarity of love, which the Father recognized on Easter morn as His own surpassing love for the lost, Christ was raised so that, in Him, believers who thus die with Him might also rise with Him.

Luther's metaphorical sacrifice of atonement, then, reflects an exchange not only of words to create this unheard-of new meaning but also of things—namely, Christ's righteousness for the sinner's sin. Christ is the Lamb of God who takes away the sin (notice: the *sin*, not the *punishment*) of the world. Such is a metaphorical atonement, not a literal one. In a literal sacrifice of atonement the priest provides a substitute to bear the punishment. But in a metaphorical sacrifice of atonement the priest offers himself to bear the sin of others in order to establish unbreakable solidarity of love with those undeserving of love. As the apostle put it, "For our sake he made him to be sin who knew no sin, so that in him we might become the righteousness of God" (2 Cor. 5:21).

For Luther, Christ in His atoning death is not a punishment-bearer but a sin-bearer. In innocence He takes on Himself the sin of the world, not as the One who does the sin, but as the One who takes responsibility for it before God. Christ's obedience in this is, as Luther puts it, a passive one; that is, He lets himself be numbered among transgressors, and so, not in place of them but with them in their place, He faces the holy wrath of God on the sin that ruins the world. And that would be the terrifying end of the story were this Christ— dead, buried, and shrouded in the sin of the world—not raised on the third day, vindicated and exalted to God's right hand of power, thence to come again. As the risen Lord, Luther's crucified and risen Christ comes to the believer ever again through the glad tidings of His Easter victory to perform His joyful exchange, so that the believer can let go of sin and die to its guilt with its crushing power. For Luther, the paradoxical good news of Christ crucified is that the believer *gets* to die with Christ in order to be raised to newness of life.

The effect of meditation on Christ's passion can be terrifying, but its purpose is not to terrorize. That would be, for Luther, a demonic abuse of this meditation. For Luther the purpose clause is crucial: God kills *in order to* make alive; God judges *in order to* justify; God mortifies *in order to* vivify. If you separate the killing, the judging, and the mortifying from the purpose of making alive, justifying, and vivifying, you do the work of unholy spirits—not of the Holy Spirit. That is why Luther hastens on in his *Meditation* to the resurrection and Christ the Victor for us, who overthrows the demonic powers by justly releasing us from the hold they have on us. The hold they have on human beings is guilt, the irrevocable facticity of evil done and good left undone by the person who in any case seeks self in all things, even in God. The devil, like the prosecuting attorney, indicts and attacks the believer with this truth of God's own and holy law to drive her to despair: "You are no disciple. You have betrayed, fled, denied, failed. You are unworthy and a disgrace." Like Peter in the Gospel of Luke, the devil wants the desperado crushed with this guilt to cry out, "Go away from me, Lord, for I am a sinful man!" (Luke 5:8).

At this juncture, Luther admonishes those who meditate on Christ's passion to claim the victory of Christ over the devil, not by denying the truth that they are sinners (in this they can "give the devil his due"), but rather by "pouring their sins back on Christ, who vanquishes them" in the joyful exchange. As a result, Luther continues, thus unburdened by Christ's own act of loving solidarity, believers can rise up afresh, stand tall and unburdened, and in faith spur themselves on to faith, for now love, not fear, has made them in their heart of hearts foes of sin who put to death their old selves. Their intentionality has been redirected; their minds have been changed and their affects reorganized. Now that they are forgiven and freed, the devil has no more rightful claim over them. One little word can fell him. Jesus has won them. He has become their new and saving Lord. Thus they actually get to arise to follow Jesus through the cross to the crown.

Note well how Luther does not play the three atonement motifs in the New Testament against one another, as if we had to choose one and reject the others, as happens so often in the history of theology. Christ died for our sins. Christ rose for our justification. We are liberated by His resurrection Spirit to follow Jesus, who loved us and gave Himself for us. Satisfaction, liberation, and imitation flow together into one harmonious account, as we shall see when we examine Luther's catechetical explanation of the second article of the Creed. Luther has us meditate on each of these aspects of the atonement and realize how they hang together in transforming us into Christians— that is, "little Christs" who become priests not for ourselves but for others in our own time and place because His prophetic Word has effectively called us to repentance and thus changed our horizon of expectation to anticipation of the public manifestation of His royal victory for us and for all.

Christ's Victory

We can dig even deeper into Luther's theology of atonement by considering his hymn "Christ Jesus Lay in Death's Strong Bands."[3] This Easter hymn, while drawing on medieval antecedents, is Luther's own composition. It is dated to 1524, early in Luther's hymn-writing career. Study of it leads us into Luther's innovative (in the Western tradition) understanding of the atonement as a mighty "duel" between life and death.

Verse 1 lays out a contradiction. On the one hand, Christ Jesus lies lifeless, imprisoned by the power of death. On the other hand, Christ Jesus is ascended and victorious at God's right hand. How is this contradiction mediated or resolved? Certainly not by a sheer act of wishful thinking, as if to say that Jesus only apparently died, that Jesus really has always been the invulnerable God, not Him truly born of Mary or truly crucified under Pontius Pilate, as if His human suffering and death were only a seeming suffering and a seeming death. Corresponding to this is a view of His death as divine play-acting, where God simply asserts the truth of our forgiveness against the false appearances of guilt and death in playacting: an artificial resurrection from an artificial death. Faith becomes a gnosis of our supposed innocence to be asserted and maintained by sheer fiat, an act of willpower in spite of the contradictory evidence of our ongoing battle with sin, death, and the power of the devil.

But in reality, when Jesus forgives sin in God's name, He does not wave a magic wand and make it disappear into thin air. Forgiveness is a moral transaction in which He takes what He forgives upon Himself so that, in the end, God holds Jesus responsible for this bold act of love for the loveless and unlovely. Thus verses 2 and 3 of the hymn explain the sense of this contradiction not merely as a verbal or rhetorical contradiction of divine playacting but as an actual contradiction between the old but truly divine judgment of death upon sin and the new surpassingly divine judgment of life upon sinners who are now found enclosed in the death of Christ, whose surpassing act of love for them overfulfills the law's just demand and in this way explodes its juridical force. Richard Massie's nineteenth-century translation of verses 2 and 3 reads as follows:

> It was a strange and dreadful strife
> when life and death contended;

the victory remained with life,
the reign of death was ended.
Holy Scripture plainly saith
that death is swallowed up by death;
its sting is lost forever.
Hallelujah!

Here the true Paschal Lamb we see,
whom God so freely gave us;
He died on the accursed tree—
so strong His love to save us.
See, His blood doth mark our door;
faith points to it, death passes o'er,
and Satan cannot harm us.
Hallelujah!

For Luther, Christ's victory is not only a matter of power, God asserting His reign against the evil usurper Death. More importantly, Christ's victory is a matter of *right* as well as might. Christ *rightfully* has won back dominion over sinners who *rightfully* had been held responsible for their sin.[4]

The idea is the Pauline one that "the wages of sin is death" such that "by the one man's obedience the many will be made righteous" (Rom. 6:23; 5:19). By descending into our place and freely, innocently, and out of surpassing love taking on Himself the sin of the world, this true Paschal Lamb of God (as we see in verse 3) removes the guilty liability of sinners, subjecting them to the dominion of Death, and thus invalidates the otherwise rightful claim of Death to condemn sinners. Christ does this *rightfully*—in uncanny Gethsemane obedience to God and out of love for sinners—by taking their sin upon Himself and thus drawing Death's condemnation rightfully to Himself. In doing so, however, Death has overstepped its bounds and condemned the one righteous man, who loved not Himself but sinners. This overreach is revealed and turned back upon Death by the risen Christ, who pronounces Death guilty and thus deprives it of its sting. Christ does this deed of exchanging Himself, the righteous for the guilty, in fulfillment of the true demand of the law to love God above all and to love one's neighbor as oneself—the neighbor who is a sinner, lost to God, hopelessly entangled in the all-too-real guilt and lethality of the world.

That is why Christ's victory is an expression not only of divine power to give life to the dead but all the more of divine *righteousness*. In the Easter victory, as Eberhard Jüngel and Ingolf Dalferth have urged, the dramatic confrontation between the Father and the Son is resolved when in the Spirit the Father recognizes as His very own this love and justice of the crucified, dead, and buried Jesus, shrouded in the sin of the world. This "recognition" is what resurrection, theologically interpreted, means: not just a physical miracle overcoming a real death but the theological miracle of God surpassing God!

We can see once again in this hymn Luther's narrative theological approach and its existential application. Luther first tells the Easter story of Christ's "strange and dreadful strife" in verses 1–3. Midway through verse 3, Luther transitions to the meaning of this narrative "for us" by recalling the exodus story of the Passover: "See, His blood doth mark our door; / faith points to it, death passes o'er, / and Satan cannot harm us."

It would be no exaggeration to say that today Christian teaching on the atonement—so crucial to any view of Christianity as a message of God's salvation, so indispensable to keeping faith from degenerating into moralism, legalism, pietism, pompous religiosity, or frenetic do-goodism—is in disarray. Very few know how to distinguish Luther's view of the "mighty duel" and the "joyful exchange" from the legalistic scheme of the so-called satisfaction theory that goes back to Anselm and that predominated in both Protestant orthodoxy and Pietism. Not to put too fine a point on it, the latter view said in effect: "You can't help but sin, but Jesus took the rap." Here Jesus is merely a punishment-bearer, a scapegoat, and the "good news" is rather a "good deal": you can escape—not your sin!—but its consequences in punishment, on the condition that you believe the right things about Jesus (so orthodoxy) or feel the right things about Jesus (so Pietism).

It is true, of course, that for Luther, Jesus faces in our place that dreadful moment of abandonment by God, expressed in the cry of dereliction from the cross. Indeed, the cry "My God, my God, why have you forsaken me!" is for Luther the test case of any true account of Christology. Jesus drinks the cup; that means He uniquely faces the wrath of God in the place of the sinners whose sins, forgiven, He takes upon Himself. Consequently, those who are baptized into His death must merely die temporally in order to be raised from death to eternal life. Jesus empties hell and shutters its doors, leaving behind the sin of the world in oblivion but leading forth in victorious procession its prisoners now freed. This teaching, so far as the uniqueness of Jesus's encounter with the wrath of God is maintained as an intradivine event between the Father and the Son, has universal implications. As the Son is truly divine, even in this utter depth of humiliation that was obedience to death, even death on a cross, the scope of His atonement is unrestricted. It is the divine election of sinful humanity to which no limits may be put. Atonement is potentially universal, for God consigned all to sin in order that He might have mercy on all (Rom. 11:32).

We cannot, however, draw from this a dogma of universal salvation. This is true for two reasons. First, the capacity to make this judgment is precisely what is attributed to Christ at His public manifestation, not to His ambassadors. It is He, not Christians, who will judge the living and the dead. Second, Christians are authorized by "the office of the keys," as it was traditionally called, to proclaim both the judgment of God and the mercy of God. Both the true threat of eternal death to God and the surpassing truth of mercy that gives life to the dead are to be sounded. And as the church makes such judgments in history, it does so prayerfully, conscientiously, and provisionally, always favoring mercy, never terrorizing.

As we have seen, the deeper truth for Luther is not that Jesus is a mere punishment-bearer but that—out of unfathomable love!—He is a sin-bearer. Rightfully then, Jesus can bring us God's righteousness, which He Himself is and enacts, to declare and to make us just; this righteousness is just who He is, as the one Man who truly lived for others, even sinful others. As the One who has claimed our sin as His own and "condemned sin in the flesh," yet who is now vindicated and victorious because He did so out of perfect love that fulfills the law's holy demand, Jesus can and does convey to us His own transformative righteousness. "For our sake he made him to be sin who knew no sin, so that in him we might become the righteousness of God" (2 Cor. 5:21).

This theme of the righteousness of God derives from the Hebrew prophets, who give voice to the LORD's controversy with His people Israel, and hence from the laments of God's suffering people, who cry out not for retribution but for God's fidelity to His promise of mercy. Luther identifies the Christian people with Israel, especially in verse 4 of his hymn "Out of the Depths I Cry to You,"[5] which says, "I hope as Israel in the Lord" (not a literal translation but a faithful lyrical paraphrase). Like so many of Luther's hymns, this hymn is a paraphrase of a psalm—in this case, Psalm 130. More generally, Luther's (at the time pathbreaking) Hebrew language exegesis and Christian theological interpretation of Old Testament texts combined to make the publication of such studies and commentaries on the Psalms bestsellers. In them the humanity of Israel in its life of yearning for God's reign and lament over its own sufferings becomes vivid and real. The Hebrew Scriptures indeed form the indispensable background of Luther's Reformation theology as his Christian "Old Testament." This particular hymn became a favorite for solemn events and indeed was sung at Luther's own funeral.

Luther and the Jews

It is fitting, then, to conclude this chapter on the cross by reflecting critically on one of the cruelest ironies attending the fate of Luther's reception in recent history: his relation to Jews and Judaism. Since the Nazi mass murder of Europe's Jews, all Christians have scrutinized their theological traditions to find and root out the spiritual sources of this unprecedented crime. Luther—an iconic figure in German history—is no exception; indeed, he is in some ways the paradigm case. The case of Luther demands particular scrutiny, since the Nazi crime occurred in the very land of Luther's reformation.

While both supporters and opponents of Hitlerism invoked the Luther image, more serious historical investigation has succeeded in clarifying the ways in which Luther's theological legacy did, and did not, open paths to the Holocaust. First of all, some historical perspective is demanded here. Luther lived some four hundred years before Nazism. A historically more direct and immediate source of religious anti-Judaism and fascism, though not racial anti-Semitism, might be found in the anti-Christian philosopher Friedrich Nietzsche. Indeed, Nietzsche's philosophical anti-Judaism—for him, Moses was the author of the repugnant "slave-morality" of resentment—was a religious source of inspiration for Nazism, which carried this diagnosis of the Jewish "malady" forward into their so-called racial science. A lot of water had flowed under the bridge since Luther's time. The theological sins that we will trace to Luther need to be historically contextualized in this fashion. Luther's own particular theological teaching was about as well known to Germans of the Nazi times as is, say, the theology of Jonathan Edwards, the Puritan divine, to Americans today—even though Edwardsian theology dominated the formative years of the United States from before the Revolution, through the Awakenings, and beyond the Civil War.

Second, as mentioned, Luther's teaching on Judaism contains a cruel irony. Luther loved the Hebrew Scriptures, the Christian "Old Testament." He earned his daily bread as a professor of Old Testament and taught himself Hebrew in order to translate the Scriptures into German from the original language. So profound was his identification with the Old Testament that he regarded the "church" as already founded in God's promise of the Messiah to Adam and Eve, and he traced the travail of the "church" as *Israel's* journey with God. Of course, this means that Luther, following Paul (who too was a Jew), regards divine promise, not instruction (torah), as the true theme of the Hebrew Scriptures, though this does not cause him to invalidate torah as God's Word—Luther published a commendable commentary on Deuteronomy!

Luther's exegesis and theological interpretation of the Hebrew Scriptures as the Christian Old Testament of promise caused him to criticize the exegesis of the rabbis, which he knew secondhand through medieval Christian commentaries. Here too we can detect not a prejudice but an actual insight. Luther, reading the Hebrew Scriptures as a narrated promise of the Messiah to come, possessed an interpretive key by which he could relativize obscure texts with clear texts. He regarded the inconclusive rabbinic debates—which, lacking this very key, seemingly insisted on the polyvalence of the scriptural text—as confused and equivocating. This harsh judgment was hardly mere bigotry. It is no accident that the pioneer of deconstruction is the Jewish philosopher Jacques Derrida, and that his central affirmation is that all writing is an attempt to capture what cannot be captured. This modernized rabbinic hermeneutic destabilizes texts taken as authoritative Scripture, which cannot function unless they deliver clear meaning to mandate and direct the community of faith that searches them. While traditional adherents of rabbinic Judaism will have their own issues with Derrida, it is the case that Luther's reading of Scripture is "Logocentric," with the Logos for him being the One who became flesh in Jesus Christ, full of grace and truth.

Luther's rejection of rabbinic commentary was thus the inevitable hermeneutical consequence of the fact that the rabbis do not see Jesus of Nazareth as the fulfillment of the Scriptures and hence the key to their clear interpretation. Thus the rabbis must be, in Luther's judgment, blind guides, who are always quarreling about the minutia of the text without coming to a conclusion in the urgent matters of God's will and human salvation. This is a trope already prefigured in the New Testament—for example, in Matthew 23's "Woe to you, scribes and Pharisees, hypocrites!" diatribe.

Third, the early Luther in fact saw through the anti-Semitic agitation of the popular papal preachers and rejected it as carnal, as we saw at the beginning of this chapter. He wrote a treatise in 1525, *That Jesus Christ Was Born a Jew*, urging political co-humanity in civil society as the prerequisite of genuine evangelization of the Jews. In today's perspective, this still seems inadequate because it presumes the self-evident superiority of Christianity as a religion over Judaism, with the goal of converting Jews. Some have gone so far as to call this "spiritual genocide," since a Jew who becomes Christian, it is thought, ceases to be a Jew. In that case Luther's friendliness toward the Jews in this early treatise is nothing more than enlightened Christendom—still a political order in which Christianity is legally normative and living Judaism is surd.

Such criticisms of the early Luther may be valid from today's perspective of American democracy and its ethos of pluralism and religious tolerance. But they should not prevent us from seeing another subtle irony. Up through the time of Nazism, the form in which Christians argued theologically for the co-humanity of Jews was, following Luther's own precedent in the 1525 treatise, to assert the human capacity of Jews for conversion to Christianity. The alternative *historically* was to argue that the Jews are irredeemable, accursed, hardened in heart, possessed by the devil. This latter caricature of the hardened and cunning Jew was the form of religious anti-Judaism to which Luther reverted at the end of his life. It was this trope that could morph into Nazi racial anti-Semitism by taking the religious theme of Jewish incorrigibility to a new, racially encoded level. Baptism, then, changes nothing, contrary to Paul's assertion in Galatians 3:26–28. Baptized or not, a Jew is a Jew is a Jew, because blood is thicker than water—so the pro-Nazi German Christians maintained.

Luther lapsed in the direction of such evil discourse at the end of his life, in the notorious tract "On the Jews and Their Lies" (1545), though we should further note that this tract was virtually suppressed after Luther's death. Nazis complained about how the Lutheran Church had suppressed Luther's "true" views on the Jews. In other words, Luther's late attack on the Jews did not in fact have significant historical influence, since it was hardly known in the intervening centuries. Indeed, up through the nineteenth century, German Jews generally celebrated Luther as the pioneer of religious freedom.

There is a danger in the foregoing of exoneration by contextualization. This is not the purpose, however, of questions about the precise "sense" that Luther's late-in-life attack on the Jews had in its own historical context. The purpose is true repentance. We ask these questions in order to identify a certain temptation, evidently latent in Christianity's own Scriptures, to which Luther succumbed, so that we can know it as a temptation and fight against it. That temptation happens when we turn the biblical metaphors into allegories or symbols of eternal truth, rather than interpret them theologically to witness to the movement of God in His grace to us.

In the first case of allegorizing timeless truths, "the Jew" becomes the fixed image of the self-justifying Pharisee, a "type" known in advance of the real experience of living and breathing Jews. In the second case of the metaphor as attesting the movement of God in grace, "the Jew" becomes you and me, as in the lyric "I hope as Israel in the Lord." Because everything written in the Scriptures was written that we might have hope, we are "the Jew," whether grafted into Israel and the covenant of promise or still zealously seeking a righteousness of our own.

In the first case, we avoid human relations with these religious others, "Jews," and substitute fixed ideas or types for human beings. At his best, Luther regularly interpreted the biblical metaphor theologically, and he was open in principle to real dialogue with Jews about the "true Israel." At his worst, Luther indulged in demonizing "the Jew" and refused to continue in the co-humanity of dialogue with real Jewish persons.

It should be noted finally, however, that Luther was an "equal opportunity" demonizer: his treatment of the Jews was cut from the same cloth as his treatment of other opponents, like the pope and the rabble-rousing agitators of the Peasants' Revolt. He saw the same devil at work in the pope, the peasants, and the Jews (others too, like the Turks and the enthusiasts). Because Luther could make no sense of his excommunication by the pope other than that the biblical prophecy of the antichrist had come true, he drew the conclusion that the devil was loosed upon the earth and that the world was about to end. And this dire inference gave license to his violent rhetoric. His verbal attacks were acts of rhetorical warfare to keep the gospel alive in the world's last, ravaged hour, as Heiko Oberman has shown us.

Two instances of literalism take place in this. The obvious one is that by the process of "demonization" the devil becomes identified with human opponents. Thus one gives up the patient way of charity in interpretation and of persistence in dialogue for warfare. Second, one takes the ultimate horizon of apocalyptic theology, the "end of the world," as a calculable chronological event. Despair over this world thus becomes theologically legitimated. Luther sinned—against his own better judgment—in both of these ways. True "Lutherans," I might add, are those who are capable of executing just such self-criticism since, as the young Luther puts it in his Romans commentary, "This is the true people of God who continually bring to bear the judgment of the cross upon themselves." Note well: *themselves*, not the other guy!

But let us return in conclusion to Luther at his best. Luther took the laments expressed in the Psalms christologically: in Israel's sorrows we taste as well the sorrows of Israel's suffering servant of the Lord, the crucified Messiah, as the cry of dereliction from the cross, quoting Psalm 22:1, demonstrates. In this way the Psalms are "Christianized," of course, but at the same time Christian theology is also "Judaized." For Luther, Jesus Christ is not only the name of the historical figure born of Mary and crucified under Pontius Pilate; He is also a corporate person who includes all Israel, as made known especially in the Psalms—even the laments to which we join our voices, crying out in eager longing for the redemption of our bodies.

PART 2

Luther's Evangelical Theology

5

Catechesis as Christian Torah

Evangelicalism after Revivalism

During the Second Great Awakening, Samuel Schmucker, the Gettysburg theologian of American Lutheranism, introduced a new method of revival to East Coast Lutherans of German origin: the anxious bench, the ancestor of today's altar call. Popularized by Charles Finney with his "new measures," the anxious bench was a seat below the preaching stage to which those who wanted to be converted came after a fire-and-brimstone sermon had motivated them to save themselves from awaiting flames down under. While immersed in the prayers of the attending ministers and the emotional singing of the congregation, surrender to God's claim was urged until the sinner broke through to the new birth.

John Williamson Nevin, a Reformed theologian and Schmucker's fellow Pennsylvanian, denounced these so-called new measures because of the "mechanical and superficial character of its earnestness. Its professional machinery, its stage dramatic way, its business-like way of doing up religion in whole and short order, and then being done with it" did not seem to him consonant with "the work and kingdom of God."[1] Such methodologies did not and could not appreciate the

99

"real meaning of the Incarnation,"[2] whereby God does the work of redemption in the hiddenness of human flesh and blood; the new measures, Nevin charged, wanted instead to bypass this hiddenness for faster, but in Nevin's judgment correspondingly ephemeral, results. In corroboration of this, at the beginning of his treatise *The Anxious Bench*, Nevin charged that the "system of New Measures has no affinity whatever with the life of the Reformation. . . . Luther would have denounced it in the most unmerciful terms." And thus, without naming names, he posed a sharp question to Schmucker: "*Why are you a Lutheran?*"[3]

Opposed to the "system of the anxious bench," Nevin urged, was the tried and true "system of the catechism." Its renewal was the goal of his treatise, as also in the Reformation before him the catechesis of the patristic church had been restored—the method adopted in the larger task of "Christianizing Christendom," as Scott H. Hendrix has forcefully argued in *Recultivating the Vineyard*.[4] "Revival," of course, had the same intention of awaking sleeping Christianity, only several centuries later and within a moribund Protestantism.

It should be noted that, no less than the revivalists, Nevin too as a theological descendant of Augustine saw new birth as the reorganization of affects such that the Christian loves God above all and all creatures in and under God. Like Luther, however, he saw this new birth as a lifelong emergence from the ashes of the old Adam, begun on baptism day but not concluded until the redemption of our bodies with the revelation of the glorious liberty of the children of God on the great day when God makes all things new. You might say that for Nevin, as for Augustine and Luther, it is not good enough to be born again once. You must be born again every new day.

In the introduction to this book, I referred to the recent *Oxford Handbook of Evangelical Theology*.[5] It contains a remarkable series of evangelical reassessments along Nevin's lines. Following Mark Noll,[6] Kevin Vanhoozer questions how much of evangelical biblicism and experientialism is rooted in Enlightenment foundationalism rather than in the Reformers or the church fathers[7]—not to mention the Bible. Robert Letham similarly observes that evangelicalism has "rarely stopped to ask whether the movement itself was a capitulation to philosophical voices from outside the church."[8] Noll charitably describes such reappraisals as evangelicalism's "coming of age."[9] Other voices are less sanguine: evangelicalism is today what it has always been, a "contested" reality (William J. Abraham).[10] Evangelicalism, especially in Britain, is a thoroughgoing adaption to secular individualism (Simon Chan).[11] "There are continuities between modern evangelicalism and the Reformation. But the discontinuities are fundamental, and their conditions were given in Britain's late seventeenth-century expanding space for religious and sectarian pluralism" (Ephraim Radner),[12] which then flourished in eighteenth- and nineteenth-century revivalism (Scot McKnight).[13]

If such historical self-knowledge with contemporary self-critique is valid, the theologians of evangelicalism appearing in this volume are united in a search for a new future "after revivalism,"[14] beyond the Calvinist-Arminian standoff[15] toward a "theology of religious experience that is grounded in the sovereign priority of God's grace and yet takes human volition seriously as Spirit-inspired response to God's initiative" (Gordon T. Smith).[16] That coordination of Word and Spirit points to a fuller trinitarianism than either Calvinism or Arminianism historically knew. Concretely and in tandem with that latter point, Gordon T. Smith argues that a fuller trinitarianism means an evangelical turn to Word and sacraments as the holy means of the Spirit.[17] What Smith argues for here, then, leads exactly to the "catechetical method" to which Nevin referred in his criticism of revivalism.

In the first part of this book, we let Luther appear in some of his lesser-known though characteristic texts through the lenses of the four historical preoccupations of evangelicalism. This introductory strategy was adopted in order to let Luther's theological profile appear in the perspective of concerns that historically have preoccupied evangelicalism. In this second part of the book, we present Luther on his own terms, according to his own doctrinal production in the "catechetical method." The evangelical theologians writing in the *Oxford Handbook* are in fact groping in this direction. While the partial lineage of evangelicalism from Luther through Arndt, Spener, and Francke is well known,[18] and this Lutheran Pietism had a role to play historically in the parallel rise of evangelicalism in Anglo-American circles, it is today Luther's rediscovered arguments against Andreas Karlstadt[19] and Huldrych Zwingli[20] that are especially at play in this volume of theologically revisionist evangelicalism.

Particularly gratifying in this connection is the essay of a grand old man of evangelical theology, Donald G. Bloesch, in the name of Luther's "happy exchange"[21] challenging the Platonic axiom that blockades deep understanding of the movement of divine compassion that took place in the atonement.[22] More broadly, and going back to the indictment of evangelicalism's uncritical absorption of early modern philosophy, there are important, if tacit, arguments going on in this volume against the authority trap of epistemological foundationalism (e.g., Abraham),[23] which eclipsed the original sense of Luther's appeal to the primacy of the gospel. Likewise, there are Luther-like arguments against evangelical biblicism, not only in Vanhoozer, as already mentioned, but also in Scot McKnight's case for "gospeling" in early Christian sacraments and creeds.[24]

Writing from the entirely different perspective of a historian of American religion, Molly Worthen in *Apostles of Reason* finds parallel flaws in modern evangelicalism, though less in its revivalism than in its inflexible and reactionary dogmatism. This maladapts evangelicalism to the discoveries of modern inquiry, which a more traditional Christian theology would receive as products of God's continuing creation. For Luther, the decisive point about the doctrine of creation is the believer's affirmation "I believe that God has created me with all that exists," meaning that creation cannot be relegated to a past act of origin but instead must be taken as God's continuing creativity and coupled to the human vocation of science—that is, "to subdue the earth and have dominion over it," as the Lord's called and appointed partners. In this framework of understanding, "Bible science" is a category mistake. The Genesis creation account is not a revealed rival to scientific accounts of cosmic origins or the origin of life. It is theology, an account of who the Originator is in the light of Israel's experience of salvation and creation in the exodus, doubled by the church's experience of salvation and new creation in the resurrection of the Crucified. Theology does not rival science but interprets it as knowledge of the Creator's works in its own light of knowledge in Christ of the Creator's will.

But it is not simply the superficial appearance of contradiction between Genesis and contemporary science that accounts for the uncritical dogmatism of evangelicalism, which would save the Bible by demonizing science. Rather, Worthen traces this dogmatism to the rationalistic deduction from perfect-being theism to biblical inerrancy. While the editor of the *Oxford Handbook* is concerned theologically sharply to distinguish evangelicalism from fundamentalism, Worthen the historian is concerned to document fundamentalism's continuing presence. The source of fundamentalism, she writes, goes back to the Protestant scholastics of the seventeenth century. "They developed a highly rationalistic method of argumentation based on the technique of the medieval Catholic scholastics. These Protestant thinkers took as their starting point the assumption—which may owe more to Christianity's roots in Greek philosophy than to any explicit teaching in the Bible—that the Supreme Being is wholly perfect and unchanging. It followed that his revelation must be perfect and unchanging too, for a perfect God who errs is a logical fallacy. He chose to reveal himself through fallible human agents, but he must have safeguarded his revelation from even the smallest error"—hence the doctrine of biblical inerrancy.[25]

This rationalistic conviction that the system of theological knowledge is founded epistemologically on the perfect revelation of the perfect being is not only circular in reasoning—not a small fault in an argument pretending rationally to found an inquiry. The worst implication, from the perspective of this study, is that it could not but render Luther's Pauline rhetorical paradox, "Christ crucified," utterly opaque, indeed an obstacle (a "stumbling block"!—see 1 Cor. 1:23). But no one can begin to articulate the gospel's claim to truth until she is able to parse the apocalyptic parables of Jesus, the preaching of "Christ crucified" by Paul, or the enigmas of John (not least concerning the "new birth," not "again" but "from above"—see John 3:3–5). The gospel is proclaimed in paradoxical ways of speaking, not clear and certain truths about ways of being that can be plucked without further ado from context, stated propositionally, and further organized into a system pretending to give a "biblical worldview." In fact, the covert processes of selection and organization in this rationalism are what really generate (or reflect) a "worldview."

The result is both the rigidity of a conscientiously closed mind against scientific discovery in theology and the sterility of supposedly "biblical" theology where the doctrine of scriptural inerrancy works as a Procrustean bed into which all the data is forced—even though Protestant competition supposedly under the banner of *sola scriptura* has produced rival and incompatible biblical "worldviews" ranging from dispensationalism to creationism.

The fundamentalism of biblical inerrancy and also the revivalist appeal to experience each in its own way reflects the internalization of early modern philosophy's obsession with securing knowledge of God on the foundation of a knowledge of knowledge (that is, on an epistemology), whether that be in the rationalist deduction of inerrancy from the idea of a perfect being or the empiricist experiential intuition of new birth. If that is so, however, the crisis in evangelical theology today cannot be met with the bromide of a supposed return to the Great Tradition. *Sola scriptura* cannot be corrected by an equally naive hermeneutic of the Great Tradition. What has been always and everywhere believed by everyone is as vague a criterion as "what the Bible says." Both sweep far too many difficulties under the rug. The Great Tradition is a recent construction that can easily be deconstructed. Even more seriously, as Christine Helmer has recently shown,[26] it substitutes another form of foundationalism in its notion of tradition, constructing a ghetto of church fideism, a sociology of knowledge that can now assume the axiomatic place previously held by rationalist deduction or empiricist intuition.

One might rather argue, as this book does, that in its concern for the new birth, evangelicalism has preserved a vital truth of Christianity, and indeed of Luther's Reformation doctrine, and has done this *better* than alternative schools of theology—yes, better than in Lutheranism itself, especially since Kant, who stigmatized affects as bigoted "inclinations" interfering with reason and duty. But the new birth is nothing other than a reorganization of affects so that the converted believer begins to love God above all and all creatures in and under God. This *fides ex corde* (as Luther put it) is not, as Kant stigmatized it, an "enthusiasm" (what an irony that Kant stole Luther's neologism from him and turned it against him!). It simply is the Spirit's coming in grace to bring the love of God into human hearts. Touched by this event of grace, human hearts are persuaded that they have indeed become the children of God and, as such, are those "born anew." Evangelicalism has understood this and preserved this for Christianity. In light of the sharp criticisms enunciated above, I trust that this deeper and more important affirmation of evangelicalism's core concern will be heard clearly and acknowledged forcefully.

What is needed, after the fall of biblical inerrancy and to avert the manipulations of the "new measures," is not a return to some other, better inerrancy (such as a "catholic" claim for "tradition," howsoever "great") but clarity about the gospel and its theology in distinction from other forms of inquiry. A tacit assumption, going back to the church father Origen (the first "systematic" theologian), is that the task of Christian theology is to use a revealed worldview to defeat the philosophers. But it seems plain that beginning with Origen it is rather the worldviews that capture theology in this procedure. Worldviews come and go; in fact, as the (too) "radically Lutheran" Rudolf Bultmann rightly noted, no one can choose a worldview, which is rather given to us by our unique place in history (or, theologically, God's continuing creation). But theology stands and falls with Jesus Christ, who "is the same yesterday and today and forever" (Heb. 13:8).

Indeed, in this light we can appreciate better how the rhetorical paradox is a subversive discourse that undermines the false security sought and found in worldviews—which are idolatries, even if they claim to be "biblical." What is needed, as Nevin diagnosed, is a better grasp of the incarnation along these lines, as the paradox of the eternal Word who became flesh to dwell among us, delivering grace and truth. That means discovery of the object of personal faith in a communication process committed to the ongoing work for teaching and preaching that is true to the gospel (Gal. 2:14), to "orthodoxy." The humble and constructive *intention* of orthodoxy (not an arrogant claim to have *achieved* it over against others) in the sense of Galatians 1:6–9 or 6:15–16, then, quite suffices for membership in this inclusive (i.e., genuinely "catholic") fellowship through the ages and across the artificial lines of today's denominations.

Faith is not faith in faith; it is not fideism, as in "You ask me how I know He lives—He lives within my heart!" The new birth is precisely not such a self-referential appeal to the evidence of one's own heart or feelings as an epistemological foundation. The new birth is faith in Jesus—an accessible phenomenon of the common world—as the Christ, the Son of God, who loved me and gave Himself for me. Such faith in this Person, moreover, is essentially social; it does not circulate within the inner recesses of "my heart" but speaks out from "heart to heart," "from faith for faith." "God has sent the Spirit of his Son into *our* hearts, crying, 'Abba! Father!'" (Gal. 4:6). Faith in Jesus Christ sings praises to God before the world in the Spirit. The doxological *audience* of this social faith's confession of Jesus Christ as Son of God is God the Father. Note well here this *trinitarian* organization of evangelical theology, which gives us the Bible not as a rationalistic foundation but as the Spirit's matrix of faith in the church's life; so Luther put it in the Large Catechism, calling the church by the Spirit "the mother who bears every believer through the Word of God." Catechesis is the method by which evangelism becomes concrete and social.

Luther's Catechism

Luther's Large Catechism is a text that became foundational in the Lutheran theological tradition by its incorporation into the 1580 Book of Concord.[27] But its origin was evangelistic. In 1528 Luther and some companions were sent to inspect the state of churches in his prince's territory, fulfilling the vacated episcopal function in regions that had officially adopted the Reformation. What Luther found appalled him: sheer ignorance of the ABCs of Christian doctrine! To address the abyss of ignorance, he composed in parallel a Small Catechism and a Large Catechism, the former for the uneducated and the latter for the instruction of ministers of the Word and sacraments.

The word "catechism" denotes the pedagogy of learning by repetition. We make fun nowadays of learning by repetition; we call it "learning by rote" and dismiss it as mindless drudgery. For many of us older ones, it brings back unhappy, even painful memories of learning multiplication tables, the periodic table of elements, conjugations of verbs or declensions of nouns in foreign languages, and so on. How much more exciting to learn by experience, to experience new things and forget the old! Stimulation comes and goes, however. It does not take root and grow. Evangelization without catechesis is like cotton candy, a quick high and then a glucose collapse. It casts the seed on rocky soil unprepared to nurture growth after the seed sprouts.

Learning by repetition is the process of *habituation* that the ancients called *paideia*, a holistic form of training mind, desire, and bodily behavior under a mentor, much as athletes still train today under coaches. If the scholars are right, this was also the form of learning in the rabbinic schools of the Judaism of Jesus's time, where pupils were also disciples, as reflected in the memorization of Jesus's sayings among disciples at the earliest, oral stage of Christian tradition. It is no accident, then, that from the beginning, and building upon its Jewish antecedents (Luther explicitly quotes Deut. 6:7–8), the church saw in catechesis the appropriate pedagogy for socializing the neophyte (the young as well as the newcomer) into the faith "so that [God's Word] may penetrate deeply into [pupils'] minds and remain fixed in their memories," as Luther puts it.

By the same reasoning, Luther retained liturgical worship to sing Sunday after Sunday the words of God into hearts and minds until they would become second nature. Indeed, Luther's Small Catechism is one that can be *prayed*, just as Luther meant it to be recited in household devotions—he regarded the home as a form of the church.[28] *Lex orandi, lex credendi*: the rule of prayer is the rule of faith, and vice versa. Adapted for Christian purposes, catechesis, whether liturgical or pedagogical, is the process of in-forming faith with texts of Scripture, the matrix of faith, which work by the Spirit to re-form the mind's ideas about God and self and so to redirect the desires of the heart.

This memorization is foundational. "It is not enough for them simply to learn and repeat these parts verbatim"; this catechetical repetition should empower learners to give a "good, correct answer when they are questioned." For Luther, that testing is not just passing an oral exam in school; rather, it is preparation for the school of life. Catechism enables one to know and confess Jesus Christ as one's hope in thick and thin. This content, as we shall see, is literally central in Luther's catechesis.

The Large Catechism, in contrast to the Small Catechism, has its doxological moments, but it can hardly be prayed. It is an *argumentative* treatise, warranting and explicating *the claims to truth* (which Luther variously called "assertions," "articles of faith," or "confessional topics") embedded in those foundational texts memorized in the catechetical tradition: the Apostles' Creed, the Lord's Prayer, and the Ten Commandments. In this sequence, Luther had inherited this selection of biblical texts from the antecedent ecumenical tradition as a minimal summation of the knowledge necessary to the adult convert preparing for baptism.

Indeed, catechesis originated in the ancient church as instruction for neophytes preparing for baptism. In the Large Catechism, Luther retrieved not only the content of catechism but also this "situation in life" as the motive for Christian learning; this motive had been obscured in Christendom, where the practice of infant baptism had been as unthinking as it was universal. Rather than leave catechetical methodology behind in the Large Catechism, as indiscriminate baptism of infants often meant, Luther extended it into adulthood, arguing for what today we call "lifelong learning." Since baptism and living as one united with Christ's death in order to rise to newness of life are precisely a matter of living life here and now, lifelong learning and increasingly sophisticated theological reflection need to accompany faith on its journey. Indeed, Luther as much as insists that no one can master the catechism in a lifetime. In the fog and friction of spiritual struggle against our sinful selves, the world, and the devil, one is always learning afresh the Ten Commandments, the Creed, and the Lord's Prayer.

For Luther, we go forward in the Christian life by always returning to the beginning, where the beginning is baptism into Christ's death and resurrection. In this context, let us note, Christian doctrine is not theory, doctrine for doctrine's sake, or dead dogma abstracted from life and preserved in a museum, or speculation that goes beyond the mandate of living in Christ to soar to unknown worlds in flights of fanciful speculation. But as baptism inaugurates the life of God's new creation in the midst of a still-hostile and unredeemed world, the baptized urgently learn what God requires of them, who God is, what God does for them, and how they are to persevere in trial and testing: "We must have [catechesis] every day in order to stand against the daily and incessant attacks and ambushes of the devil with his thousand arts."

Since Christian faith is never something that occurs naturally to us, it must be learned—again and again and again. "All the prophets and all the saints have had to learn it, but they have always remained pupils, and they must continue to be so." This is so because the Word of God is always an event for us, never something we master and possess like an acquired trait, but rather the saving event that masters us—again and again—in life and in death.

At the very center of Luther's Large Catechism is his account of how Jesus Christ, the incarnate Word of God, has become "my Lord." Jesus becoming our Lord is the saving event that overtakes us, like Saul on the road to Damascus—*this* is *the* Word of God that catechesis aims to teach us. "The advantage of Luther's Catechism as a life book—and not so much a text book—will only show well in succeeding to pull Christian faith deeply into life and conversely to immerse life in the fountain of Christian faith."[29]

The stewardship of this event is entrusted "especially to us who want to be pastors and preachers." Their auditors—that is, the rest of the Christian community—also have their responsibility: to support this public ministry of Word and sacrament and, further, critically to judge its fidelity by the same knowledge of the same catechism. The pastoral ministry is the community's ministry *to* Word and sacrament; it sees to it that this comprehensive and inexhaustible event of learning about God centered in Christ is and remains central to this community's way of life in the world. Luther does not mince words in judging lazy and negligent preachers who have not cracked a theological book or striven to grow theologically since graduating from seminary. He says such preachers in fact exploit their parishioners, "living off the fat of the land," acting more as "swineherds and keepers of dogs than guardians of souls and pastors." Of course, this same sharp judgment also falls on lazy and negligent auditors, who demand that pastors be cheerleaders and hand-holders and CEOs and glad-handers—anything but ministers of Word and sacrament.

A turn away from catechesis creates a vacuum in the congregation; this vacuum is filled with a bundle of contradictory expectations from the surrounding culture that rip poor pastors to pieces. If congregations do not knowingly expect their pastors to be learned in Scripture and Christian doctrine—as apt teachers who are encouraged and given time to study so that parishioners can in turn be taught Jesus as saving Lord in the complexities and challenges of the day—why are they surprised when pastors act like feckless politicians, if not Luther's "lazy bellies," rather than guardians of souls and pastors of flocks? Perhaps they don't *want* to be one flock under one shepherd, engaged in battle with sin, death, and the power of the devil! Then it is time to preach the new birth until the soil is prepared again by the Spirit to receive the seed of the Word of God!

As mentioned, Luther inherited from the ecumenical past the three parts of the catechism—the Creed, the Lord's Prayer, and the Ten Commandments—in that order: "the three parts that have been in Christendom from ancient days," a "brief summary and digest of the entire Holy Scriptures." These three texts "contain what every Christian should know." Indeed, he continues, "anyone who does not know [the catechism] should not be numbered among Christians or admitted to any sacrament." For the radical hospitality of the God of the gospel consists in holy baptism, the bath that washes the newcomer in welcoming her to the meal on the way to the messianic feast to come. And this radical hospitality is at work by the Spirit in the catechetical transformation of the mind's ideas about God, self, and world and the reform of the heart's desires by the new birth to love God above all and all creatures in and under God.

That is the sense, by the way, of the Lutheran custom of catechetical instruction before admission to the Lord's Table. In a church that baptizes infants, the catechesis that adults would have received is postponed until a child can understand and answer for herself. Then she can be admitted to the Lord's Supper, when she knowingly and publicly can confirm her baptism. While there is no obligation to follow this custom legalistically, we should appreciate its rationale: catechesis is preparation for baptism, as baptism is preparation for the Lord's Supper, as the Lord's Supper is preparation for the messianic feast to come. Today these preparations are matters of lifelong learning. The sequence is not arbitrary but plots the gospel narrative into every human life.

Within this ecumenical tradition and consensus concerning the Commandments, the Creed, and the Lord's Prayer, Luther innovated in one simple but profound stroke. As Luther grasped that catechesis is Christian "torah"—that is, instruction for the life of the baptized—he also saw that the new and Christian life proceeds *in sequence* from death to sin to resurrection to newness of life, from cross to new creation. He accordingly reorganized the traditional sequence of teaching the texts to reflect this law-gospel ordering.[30] The traditional sequence (Creed, Lord's Prayer, Ten Commandments) suggested to him that Christian dogma led to a new law and a superior piety in which believers make themselves worthy of grace. Luther's new sequence (Ten Commandments, Creed, Lord's Prayer, and the sacraments of baptism and the Lord's Supper, which he added here as the Spirit's resources for living the Lord's Prayer) suggests, as we shall see, that Christian life is the effect of God's new creative command in which God makes believers become in power what they already are in principle, His righteousness in Christ before the world.

Thus the Commandments, detailing what the Creator expects of His creatures, precede the other texts in order to show the lost human state of impotence and need. Working despair of the existing self by the demands of the law is God's holy work, as the Judge already now anticipating the Last Day. The law's *demand* brings about a "terrifying" realization, yet one that is effected for the sake of an infinitely more consoling one—namely, of what God *gives* in creation, its redemption and fulfillment, as summarized in the Creed. Consequently, the Creed is no longer an unintelligible revealed dogma taken on ecclesiastical authority, but gospel articulately telling of God at work for us re-creating our lost world. Thus gifted with new life, "sanctification" is not a new legalism or pietism, a renewed attempt to make oneself worthy of grace. Such an endeavor would in fact be a fall from grace, turning the gift of God into a merited reward. Rather, grace ever remains an utterly free gift and thus an ever-new event through the twists and turns of life, from baptism day to resurrection day. Sanctification in this light is itself grace at work, understood and explicated as *holy secularity*: daily life *in the world* lived consciously and conscientiously before God, the Father in heaven, in unity with His Son, at whose invitation believers pray in the power of their Spirit, as we shall see in detail in the next chapters.

6

The Decalogue

Luther's Christian Reading of the Law

You might notice straight off that Luther dispensed with the prologue to the Decalogue,[1] "I am the LORD your God, who brought you out of the land of Egypt, out of the house of slavery." This is not an inconsequential edit. The prologue provides the *ergo*, the grounding, of the injunction following: "Have no other gods"—that is, gods who will bring you back again to bondage. Because God is the liberator, what follows are directives for the life of the liberated people of God, "that your days may be long and that it may go well with you in the land that the LORD your God is giving you."

What has Luther done by removing this prologue that has proved to be so important for modern scholarship's assessment of the Ten Commandments? Have we here, one might fear, an instance of Luther's anti-Judaism overriding the plain sense of the text? Or of his social conservativism blunting the force of the Bible's message of God's solidarity with the poor and the oppressed? It has been alleged, for example, that in his Small Catechism "Luther dropped the politically concrete preamble of the Decalogue . . . [and] extended the command to honor one's parents to authorities as such. These two symptomatic

113

changes of the scriptural basis of Luther's most influential catechism are indicative of how Lutheranism became prone to obedience and subservience toward any established order, including severely unjust ones, instead of being faithful to the God of liberation (sola fide) and standing in solidarity with the downtrodden."[2] Is it so? What hath Luther wrought?

There are truths contained in this critique, particularly if we fail to make any distinction between what Luther taught and how he lived, on the one hand, and what historical Lutheranism after him made of Luther's legacy under the exigencies of the Counter-Reformation and the Wars of Religion, on the other. But let us try to understand Luther in his own right. Why, according to his own lights, did Luther drop the biblical prologue to the Decalogue? The simple answer is that, historically and critically, the prologue is addressed not to gentiles in the year 1528 but to ancient Israelites. What is addressed to gentile Christians is the gospel, which to be sure brings along with it the Scriptures of Israel. What is at issue here, then, is epistemic access and the corresponding hermeneutic by which gentile Christians read Israel's Scriptures as their "Old Testament."

In the years before Luther wrote the catechisms, attempts in the name of reformation to establish and enforce biblical law in place of local traditions of law had been undertaken by Luther's former colleague Andreas Karlstadt and then by his former protégé Thomas Müntzer. Karlstadt saw in Luther's distinction of law and gospel a false differentiation that reformed the church but left the state and society immune from the criticism of biblical law. So Karlstadt wanted to apply biblical law to Saxon Germany, beginning with the iconoclastic destruction of "graven images"—the statues and paintings in the churches. Müntzer took things a "radical" step further when he argued that Karlstadt's biblicism mistook the letter for the spirit of the law, which he proclaimed was "revolutionary." Could not, he wondered, the prologue to the Decalogue give holy sanction to revolutionary violence against the established order, as it seems to have done, for example, in the book of Joshua?

The spirit of the law, Müntzer thus came to proclaim, was revolutionary violence against the oppressive powers that be. In a notorious
sermon on the book of Daniel delivered to the princes, Müntzer,
drawing from the genocidal campaigns in Joshua, proclaimed the
chilling words "The godless have no right to exist."[3] Responding to
this provocation in a tract that itself became notorious, Luther turned
the tables to argue in effect that neither do insurrectionists have a
right to exist. After fomenting the Peasants' Revolt with promises
of armies of angels coming from heaven to the aid of the untrained
farmers and herders rising up against the trained armies of the princes,
Müntzer himself suffered the sword that he had taken up in 1525. In
Zurich just a few years later, Luther's rival in reformation, Huldrych
Zwingli, suffered a similar fate while leading an army to war in 1531.
Surveying the Christian carnage of attempting to enforce biblical law
on unbelievers, Menno Simons recoiled from these violent appropria-
tions of holy war from ancient Israel and led the Anabaptist movement
into a principled life of separation from the powers that be (as well
as the powers that would be), where in a disciplined subculture true
Christians could live according to biblical law.

Such were the options, played out in dramatic contemporary history, that Luther saw before him when he undertook his explanation
of how and in what ways biblical law binds the Christian. It was in this
nexus of concerns that Luther omitted the prologue to the Decalogue.
After all, he reasoned, it is not us gentiles whom the LORD rescued
from the land of Egypt; nor was the consequent positive law that
Moses provided the liberated Israelites addressed to other peoples.
The book of Deuteronomy, closely and properly read, repeatedly
stresses that all the precepts that are written must be kept without
exception if blessings, not curses, are to fall upon the covenanted
people of God. The apostle Paul in Galatians warned against gentiles
submitting to circumcision because it entailed just this Deuteronomic
consequence and therefore would put the Galatians under the curse
of the law (Gal. 3:10, which picks up on a repeated injunction in
Deuteronomy, e.g., 27:26). What we have in biblical law, then, is the
record of the civil code for that time and place in ancient Israel. It

is, Luther wrote, the Jewish *Sachsenspiegel* (the legal code and case history of the Saxons). It is therefore *not* addressed to us gentiles and does not and should not bind us, unless we are to convert to Judaism. Levitical law is not Christian Sharia but Israelite jurisprudence as later filtered by normative or rabbinic Judaism.

Sometimes theologians try to distinguish the categorical prohibitions of the Decalogue from the conditional case laws of the legal code, arguing that the former "moral" law remains binding as opposed to the ceremonial and civil law of ancient Israel. Not so fast, Luther replies; not even the Ten Commandments bind us insofar as they belong as part to the whole of ancient Israelite law. Thus Luther not only edits out the prologue from the Catechism, but for identical reasons he also (1) drops the prohibition of images, (2) de-literalizes the Sabbath commandment in light of Jesus's controversies of healing on the Sabbath and the Christian innovation of worshiping on Sunday as the Lord's Day of the resurrection, and (3) sharply critiques the commandments against coveting for regarding wives and domestic servants as property. Luther can appropriate the Ten Commandments for us today only by way of such gospel revisionism!

But this by no means implies an antinomian slackening of the law's holy demand. Luther interprets the Ten Commandments in the light of Jesus's Sermon on the Mount, which both radicalizes the negative prohibitions into positive commands to love and focuses a divine spotlight on the motives for obedience in the heart, which the heavenly Father sees in secret and knows in secret. To be sure, this intensification and radicalization of the law in the Sermon on the Mount also has Jewish sources in the prophets, who proclaim the LORD as a Judge who searches and judges the heart. Luther sees this and sees how it further implies a critique of the Pharisaic and later rabbinic strategy of "building a fence around the law"—that is, adding regulations that inhibit violations of the letter of the law. The most famous of these is the Jewish practice of avoiding pronunciation of the divine name, the holy Tetragrammaton, and substituting for it the title "Adonai" (NRSV: LORD). The reasoning is that if one never utters the divine name YHWH, one can never be guilty of taking the name in vain.

We gentile Christians, Luther argues, appropriate the Decalogue of Moses (and indeed the rest of the Old Testament law), then, through the lenses of the Sermon on the Mount, which makes motivation before God crucial to true obedience, and through Paul's teaching in Romans 12–14, which makes the love shown in Christ, who fulfilled the law for those unworthy, the key to all the commandments. Where modern scholarship sees a gulf emerging between Matthew and Paul, Luther's anti-antinomian doctrine of justification by faith on account of Christ's obedience sees complementary emphases. We gentile Christians may receive the revised Decalogue of Moses, then, as a much clearer statement of the natural law indelibly written on the human heart (Rom. 2:12–16), manifested in the conscience's conflicting judgments obscured by sinfulness. But the law's requirement is now made clear in the light of Christ, who fulfilled the law by loving God above all in selflessly loving the unworthy to the point of death—even death on a cross (Phil. 2:8).

What takes the place of the historical prologue? As the root and source of all the other commandments, Luther holds, the first commandment has us not only eschew idols but, positively, cling to the "one true God." In place of the liberating act of the exodus for ancient Israel, Luther grounds or justifies the commandments on the "natural law," which requires reasonable creatures to put all their fear, love, and trust in the "one true God."

This notion of the one true God might easily be misunderstood today as an assertion of religious superiority, as if our tribal deity were the true one and all the others false. It requires careful examination to understand that Luther has something else entirely in mind; indeed, he is trying, with the notion of the one true God, to get past the tribal warfare of the gods. Just as the prophets of Israel matured to the teaching that as true God, the LORD can judge His own people when they turn Him into their national idol (cf. Amos 3:2), Luther pits the one true God against the idols manufactured in the religion business for chauvinistic purposes. As he will say later, if we believed the one true God, we would hardly be confirmed in our sense of religiously sanctioned nationalistic superiority to others. This belief would rather "terrify us."

What has happened in deleting the prologue is this: the *henothe-istic* first commandment of Israel—not to set up the idols of other gods before the empty throne of the ark of the covenant, the seat of the invisible LORD in the tabernacle—becomes in Luther's Christian rereading (but also in Jewish rereadings, as, for example, in Second Isaiah) the command of radical *monotheism*[4] to not fear, love, or trust anyone or anything less than the one and only true God—that is, the *One who is Creator of all that is other than God*, the unique and incomparable God of all. That is neither a Jewish tribal God nor a Christian tribal God. Only such a Creator of all things "out of nothing" qualifies as the one true God. This is the God who is the eternal fountain of generosity, who gives without any need of return (though in the return of creatures' praise and thanksgiving to the one true God lies their own great good). This God who does not need us but rather gives all is "the one, eternal good," whose gifts may only be received and blessed with thanksgivings that do not separate the gifts from the Giver but in all things give the glory to God alone, *soli Deo gloria*. Salvation, then, is just this "boasting in the Lord."

This notion of the one true God grounds Luther's remarkable ex-ploration into what it means "to have a God"—namely, as something more like "being had" or "being captivated." Whatever captures desire at its seat in the human heart is one's operational deity. To "have" a God, then, is like all kinds of other "having" in that something becomes my own, my very own, in an act of personal appropriation, as in "He or she becomes my beloved."[5] But to "have" God is not like any other kind of possession in the world of creatures, since God is not a creature alongside others but the one true Giver of all creatures. This in turn makes all created things, including the self, gifts of God to be received with joy and thanksgiving and the kinds of love that variously befit these various gifts. Food is to be consumed with relish; the spouse is to be embraced with joy.

In contemporary English we say that we "love" our spouses, our children, our craft beer, our video games. But all these various goods are desired in varying ways, and these loves are accordingly prioritized. There is a hierarchy of loves, which Luther, following Augustine's teaching on the *ordo caritatis*, embraced. Sometimes this hierarchy is explained in a hostile way, as denying enjoyment to lesser goods, which are merely to be used. But lesser goods are suffused with God the Giver, whose gifts they are, so that the use of them may be enjoyed in God. The sharp contrast between enjoyment and use surfaces only when lesser goods—that is, created things—are loved with the love that God the Creator alone deserves and satisfies.

To have God "the Giver," then, is to fear at last only God's disapproval, to value or esteem God's approval above all, to trust that God's approval is generous and merciful and endures forever. To have God is the kind of having that the "heart" has, which can never possess its beloved like a thing to be used, but rather can "have" God in fear, love, and trust above all others. Having God in this way of being had by the One who truly gives all, then, entails loving all creatures in and under God as also gifts from God, just as the second table of the Ten Commandments goes on to elaborate. By contrast, then, not having One who is truly God entails making gods of one's possessions, greedily hoarding them, and justifying one's greed in the name of rational, even enlightened self-interest. A merely negative civil righteousness, then, which does not visibly trespass the prohibitions, can conceal a self that is greed personified. Or, as in Jesus's parable, it can conceal a "fool" who puts an infinite burden of desire on a finite treasure that cannot but fail. The human world is littered with gods that have failed.

Three final "apocalyptic" notes on the first table of the law. First, Luther acknowledges the apparent contradiction in experience between all that he has taught about having only the one true God and the bitter observation that the righteous suffer and the wicked prosper. Faith—having God, having the one true God as one's only eternal good—is often, he observes, in contradiction to experience of the world, where the innocent suffer and the wicked prosper. So the mature witness of Israel's Wisdom tradition in the book of Job, like that of Second Isaiah, comes to bear on Luther's Christian revision of the Decalogue. Faith in the one true God necessarily points forward from the bitter experience of actual evil, which contradicts

God's revealed will, to a divine future still invisible in the present, groaning under structures of malice and injustice. The just live by faith in the one true God, as Habakkuk (whom Paul the apostle cites in Rom. 1:17; see Hab. 2:4) teaches—in *hope*, then, of the coming of God's reign, the full, powerful, and visible implementation of the first commandment, putting an end once and for all to the gods that fail.

Second, present appearances of the prosperity of the wicked and the suffering of the righteous, as if the whole of the story, are correspondingly exposed in truth as the lies that the devil spins to deceive, going all the way back to the seduction "You will not die! But you will be like God, knowing good and evil!" That is why if we, unwitting but willing pawns of the serpent, were to believe in the one true God, it would "terrify us," so deeply is this faith in God in contradiction to the actual way we live, quite settled down and at home within structures of malice and injustice that usurp the reign of the One who is truly God.

Third, we began this chapter by asking if we today need to "radicalize" the Reformation. Indeed we do, though not in the way suggested by the Radicalizing Reformation project with its ninety-four theses.[6] Luther tried to reform Christendom in his day. That project is over, but Luther's theology of holy secularity abides. In place of Christendom, we need to think today of the coming of the Beloved Community of God.[7] The second table of the Decalogue spells out the corresponding social dimensions.

If the God who gives all things to all creatures is our one and only eternal good—that is, alone the One worthy of captivating the whole desire of our hearts to the cause of His eternal reign—then the world of His gifts is the site of sanctification, the place where the love of this God transpires for His creatures in all sorts of specific ways: social, familial, economic, legal, and personal. Secular life (that is, life in this passing world—individually our temporary and spatially delimited span within it marked by our bodily organism, socially our nations and empires that rise and fall) is the place given for holy and creative labor in fulfillment of the image of God. Here on the earth we are made in the image of God for the sake of acquiring likeness to God.

The common body is the object of God's creative and redemptive love, so also of those renewed in the image of God, who is Jesus Christ, the new Adam. The moral revolution effected by Luther's theological reordering of the catechetical texts was to move sanctification from the individualistic struggle to get to heaven by religious works to the corporate struggle to remake this earth as a structure of justice animated by love and effected by truly good works.

Truly Good Works

In exposition of the largely negative prohibitions of the Ten Commandments, Luther in his Christian rereading and appropriation of the second table amplifies, if not inserts, the positive injunctions implied: not to commit adultery entails honoring and cherishing the spouse; not to steal means to defend the neighbor's property and help in every need; not to bear false witness means to make true witness, especially in preaching God's Word; not to covet means to cultivate generosity; not to kill means to defend and preserve life. This doing of good is the truly "good" work in contrast to self-invented religious works masquerading as good works.

In the commentary on the second table, Luther thus regularly contrasts the "self-invented" works of the religion business with the "divine commands" of the Creator directed to the good of the earthly life, here and now, of His creatures. The "self-invented" works of religion are in fact diabolic attempts to subvert the divine command, as Luther sees paradigmatically in the serpent's deception of the mother of us all, "Has God really said?" Sowing doubt about the Creator's commandment for life, the serpent insinuates jealousy on the part of God and so inspires envy in the first couple, offering to the creature the prospect of attaining the power and knowledge that God supposedly wants to keep for Himself. So Luther interprets the religious works of fasting, sexual abstinence, pilgrimages, and vows, along with the cults of relics and saints and so on, as demonic subversions of the divine command for life (Gen. 1:26–28). All these "self-invented" acts of self-abnegation to earn heavenly reward are deceptions of the devil to steer humanity away from the Creator's gift of temporal life and the commandments that safeguard its well-being on the way to the coming of the Beloved Community.

Moreover, Luther's apocalyptic theology knows that this struggle of love for justice in society and on the earth, commanded by the Creator in the commandments, is in dead earnest; that the enemy of God figured in the cunning serpent is vicious and powerful; and that Christ must reign as One in battle until He defeats all enemies. Luther's Christian ethic of faith active in love and in hope for the world is not utopian or idealistic but realistic—at times crudely realistic—as Luther sees (with the prophets of Israel and Augustine's ruminations in his *City of God*) historical events as God using one sinner to constrain and punish another.

Luther's ethic is not an easy, optimistic confidence in the inevitable progress of the human race but a hope against hope in a world always on the cusp of self-destruction, aided and abetted by the religion business and its marketing of stratagems of spiritual escapism, false comfort, and easy conscience. But the second table refocuses attention to this world in its often desperate daily needs. Here is the site of sanctification, in the common body, as "holy secularity": in the family, on the job, in school, in trade and governance—even in organized religion! Luther's exposition of the second table gives the reader a "social gospel" or a Christian social ethics in outline.

We can connect this with Luther's teaching on the "three estates" or, as Bonhoeffer later put it, the "mandates of creation." These "estates" are derived from the analysis of Genesis 1:26–28, the divine command to the human couple to have dominion over the earth in analogy to (as the reflection or image of) the LORD's creative and loving dominion over the cosmos. The second table, in this light, is not some kind of arbitrary list of rules revealed from heaven but a kind of basic sociology, a "natural law" description of human communal life on the earth, with the responsibilities therewith incumbent on all who enjoy life within human community and seek their own welfare in the community's welfare. The commandments are a "summary of the essential demands made in conditions of life where life is not a power possessed but a gift received in relationships with the Creator, other creatures, and, implicitly, the creation."[8] The commandments thus protect the fundamental institutional structures of social existence: the family, the economy, cultural exchange, public worship, and the legal order. Early Lutheran theology thus taught what John Witte calls a kind of "Christian republicanism,"[9] which is based on three "institutional" mandates: the command to rule (governance), the command to be fruitful and multiply (the family as domestic economy), and the command to give thanks to God for the gifts of life (public worship).

For us today there are several important problems with early Lutheranism's now-outdated sociological formulations of Christian "republicanism."[10] Chiefly problematic is historical Lutheranism's post-Reformation project of a rival version of Christendom over against that of Roman Catholicism; this became stamped, if not warped, by the exigencies of the Counter-Reformation and the Wars of Religion. The problems are these. First, does the mandate to govern entail uncritical obedience to the political sovereignty of the state? Second, what are we to make of the modern separation of the family from the economy, as if the family were a "haven in the heartless world" while the supposedly autonomous economy is now governed by the supposedly natural law of the market, which is after the rationalization of the prosperity of the fittest?

The reader will see that in his treatment of the fourth commandment, Luther derives all authority from the natural care that parents have for their children; the pre-political head of household (a very extended family that functions also as an economic unit) is the source of all other genuine authority—for example, teachers and educators, princes and governors, apostles and pastors, elders and the experienced, experts and scientists. Yet such authority in a fallen world has become coercive, as the curses in Genesis 3 attest.

Thus, as Oswald Bayer observes, Luther was never willing to regard the state, taken now as political sovereignty, as an order of creation.[11] It is rather a *Notordnung*, "an emergency order," even a legally established "state of exception" (so Giorgio Agamben in his exposé of Hobbes's *Leviathan*)[12] in which, by divine forbearance, some violent sinners constrain other violent sinners by means of the state's arbitrary monopolization of the means of coercion. This unstable institution cannot, therefore, analogize the reign of God. It is temporary and will pass away when God reigns in fullness of power and glory (compare this to Samuel's speech in 1 Sam. 8). It is in the interim the unsteady surrogate of God's *alien* work, which God does *paradoxically* for the sake of His *proper* work.

Yet, at the same time, God's mandate to the human couple to rule the earth abides, just as creation continues and God acts providentially both to preserve what He creates and to move the creation onward to His own overarching goal. Creation most fundamentally continues in procreation. The assumption of the biblical text, as also of Luther, is that the human couple that is blessed with fertility is not a private relation of secret lovers but a public estate as well as an economic unit. In this way it is also, in the Bible and for Luther, the basis of society and the source of all genuine earthly authority. The care of children until they in turn mature as caretakers in a covenant of the generations is the model of genuine authority, which is not only or even chiefly the legal order of a given state (of exception!).

It is difficult to square this notion, expressed in Luther's expositions of the fourth and sixth commandments, with modern ideas of private sexual intimacy for the pursuit of pleasure cordoned off from attendant social responsibilities, let alone from the competitive relations of economic life.[13] Today, sex too is commoditized in pornography, predation, human trafficking, the reduction of marriage to a contract relation, the bioengineering of children, sex-selective abortion, the sale of fetal body parts, and so on. Indeed, a powerful argument could be made that the economic imperative of contemporary corporate capitalism for the sake of profit maximization *must* dismantle the classical household economy in order to remake workers into impersonal, degenderized individuals and thus readily replaceable cogs in its machinery. In any case, as working pastors know from sad experience, the contemporary family is hardly a "haven in a heartless world."[14] Nowhere does the contemporary economic order penetrate with more profound damage than into this "haven."

In any event, we ought to see in Luther's exposition of the second table marching orders for us in our own times: to scope out truly good works on the earth and in society under the rubric of holy secularity, rather than a once-for-all imposition of a fixed and immutable social order. Here on the earth and in time is the site of sanctification in the human body, bound together with other human and animal bodies in a common body, the ecosystem. The various dimensions of social life protected in the commandments of the second table direct us to "arenas of responsibility" (Robert Benne) for the care and redemption of all that God has made. Here, for Luther, a true saint is to be found who patiently bears with others, even fools and enemies, giving over the reckoning to the LORD when suffering cruel injustice, and never giving up on the infinity of truly good works commanded by God the Creator for the sake of life.

7

The Creed

The Creed's Trinitarian Structure

For Luther, one comes to *know* God by receiving with joy and thanksgiving His gifts, up to and including especially the gift of a share in His own eternal life of Triune community through union with Jesus Christ.[1] The Creed tells us what we are to *know* about God, since knowledge is power, and the power in question is the power to become children of the heavenly Father in union with the Son and so to live as beloved children of God. To be sure, this is no ordinary knowledge that in its scientific objectivity brackets out the subjectivity of the person who knows. Rather, it is extraordinary knowledge that gives the object of knowledge, Jesus Christ and the Triune God, by impartation of the Spirit of God forming a new subjectivity. The Spirit works trusting faith in Christ in His personal promise to be there for us; the Spirit does this by way of proclaiming the joyful exchange of human sin for Christ's righteousness. In just this way of an extraordinary nuptial of Christ and faith, the Spirit transforms the human subject. This yields the Hebrew kind of knowledge of God imparted to faith—"a mighty, living active thing"—just as Spirit-given faith is a patiency operative in love.

For centuries the Apostles' Creed had been divided into twelve articles, each one supposedly having been contributed by one of the original twelve apostles so that they would have a uniform doctrinal statement before setting out on their separate ways. It is interesting to reflect on the hermeneutical supposition involved in this artificial organization of the Creed into twelve parts; such reflection helps us to appreciate all the more Luther's retrieval of the original baptismal context of the Creed and thus also its *trinitarian* structure.

The twelvefold division reflected a concern for the authority of a linguistically uniform formulation of the faith, historically grounded in the supposed fact of an original apostolic consensus. The idea was that whatever local customs and diverging vocabularies or theological conceptualities developed later on, the original faith of the apostles was deposited and available in a standard, clearly enunciated formulation. This concern for mere authority and merely linguistic uniformity invested in the exact formulation of the Creed, however, does not correspond to historical reality. Nor does it actually appreciate the Creed's true contribution: defining Christian faith as baptism by Spirit-given union with the Son into the eternal life of the Triune God. To appreciate this actual role of the early baptismal creeds, one would do better to study the second-century church father Irenaeus, the knowledge of whom was just becoming available during Luther's time.[2]

The Apostles' Creed, derived from the old Roman baptismal creed, became the standard liturgical creed in the Western Latin churches because of its role in the conversion of human subjectivity that takes place in sacramental baptism. The threefold profession is made of the Father who sends, the Son who is sent, and the Holy Spirit who unites the believer with the Son by repentance and faith, so that she may live before Him now and forever. By this narrative summation, the Creed articulates the unity of creation, redemption, and fulfillment, as Luther (following Irenaeus, whether he realizes it or not) sets it against every form of gnostic dualism (including the modern dualism of the spheres of creation and redemption that Bonhoeffer attacked as "thinking in terms of two spheres"[3]): "God has created us for no other reason than to redeem us and bring us to Himself" (Large Catechism). With this dynamic trinitarian unity of the Old and New Testaments, Luther frames the preaching of God's Word as law and gospel by the Pauline purpose clause "God has imprisoned all in disobedience *so that* he may be merciful to all" (Rom. 11:32).

Newness of Life

With its first-person personal pronoun, "I believe" (in distinction from the "We believe" of the Nicene Creed), liturgical recitation of the Apostles' Creed works to reinforce the ongoing baptismal transformation of the believing subject as one who has died with Christ to sin in order to rise up daily to newness of life. Thus, in Luther's exposition the individualizing *pro me* (for me) nature of appropriating faith is continually underscored: "I believe that God has created *me*. . . . I believe that Jesus Christ is *my* saving Lord. . . . I believe that the Holy Spirit has called *me* by the gospel." (The "we" of the Nicene Creed, by contrast, works to identify communities of faith united in the confession of the true and full deity of the Son, "of one being with the Father"; it is an ecclesial creed that reflects an ongoing decision for orthodoxy against the Arian deviation.)

Sometimes nowadays it is urged that Luther, unlike Melanchthon, had no use for a so-called third use of the law—that is, not only to curb sin politically or to reveal sin theologically but also, positively, to guide the believer in newness of life. Whatever semantical subtleties are involved here in the differences between Luther and Melanchthon (and Calvin), Luther cannot be more explicit in the Large Catechism in saying that the Creed, telling us what God does for us and gives to us, enables us to fulfill the Ten Commandments. The reason for this purpose clause has to do with the aforementioned unity of the Testaments. The Spirit who brings us to the Father is the same Spirit who sees to the law's fulfillment in the redeemed; indeed, these two are inseparable aspects of the same reality of salvation. For salvation is not only the forgiveness of guilt on account of Christ—that is, justification already now and peace with God. But this very salvation has a future "hope of righteousness" (Gal. 5:5) that consists in loving God above all and all creatures in and under God. This love is the fulfillment of the commandments.

For there is only one true God, so that all that God does for us in the Creed cannot but return us to the first commandment. The first commandment, in turn, can function as demand ("Have no other gods") or promise ("I am the LORD your God"), depending on the context and the audience. Luther expounds the first article of the Creed to bring out its deep correspondence to the first commandment: we are to have no other gods *because* only the One who is Creator of all that is other than Himself can *truly* help in every time of need. We should learn from the first article, then, that no one has life in and of herself, but instead that each and every life is given, nurtured, and preserved in God's continuous act of creating. If we were to realize this, we would see that we are duty-bound to acknowledge joyfully our continuing dependence on God along with our interdependence with God's creatures in praise and thankful obedience to this heavenly Father's goodwill. To live accordingly would be to love God above all and all creatures in and under God. Just so, Luther notes, "if we believed this article it would terrify us," exposing as it does our human failure and so driving us on to God's further works of redemption and fulfillment.

Why would knowledge of God's goodness in creation and our debt of gratitude "terrify" us? Believing is not merely holding theoretically to the beliefs listed in the Creed, but using these beliefs knowledgeably to interpret our experience, so that love and desire for God, who gives all things, is kindled in our hearts. But in fact we are full of doubts and fears, resignation and apathy, always on the cusp of spiritual despair. Taken seriously, taken existentially, taken *pro me* all the way down to the core of our beings, we come by way of these beliefs to a terrifying insight into our wayward hearts: that our actual lives of unbelief rob God of the praise we owe, just as they rob neighbors of the love they need from us, while depriving the world of the hope we ought to have for our labors of love in it as God's creation destined for redemption and fulfillment.

But how can love for God who gives in continuous creation be kindled in the heart that is thus alienated and, if truthfully self-aware, uneasy in conscience and not at peace with God? Only by turning to the second article, telling of the heavenly Father's Son, who completely gives Himself to me, the helpless sinner, in order to become my saving or redeeming or liberating Lord. Luther holds together all three of the traditional accounts of the saving work of Christ (satisfaction of God's wrath, liberation from demonic powers, and moral example) and weaves them together into a whole. He does not pit one motif against the others. Christ is our liberator from the demons, our reconciler with God, and the trailblazing pioneer for us to follow as disciplined children of God, "disciples." "In Christ God shows Himself as He really is and breaks through the ambiguous (promising or threatening) image that is pending about Him in the Commandments."[4]

Certainly, in this interlocking whole of New Testament teachings about the redemption that is in Christ Jesus, Luther puts the price Christ paid with his "holy, innocent, and precious blood" at the center of the atonement motifs; this is the high cost paid by the humble Son of God for what I, the proud creature, owed. The economic language of debt and its satisfaction is employed here in order to be fulfilled and so overcome by the exchange that is not a calculated quid pro quo but a surpassingly lavish exchange of life for death and righteousness for sin. Christ fulfilled and indeed surpassed the law by loving God above all in obediently loving unworthy sinners more than Himself. Rightly understood as the gracious initiative of the God who gives, this sacrifice of atonement is the christological basis, Luther avers, of the Reformation's doctrine of justification by faith. Christ gives us His righteousness only by taking on Himself our sinfulness. Only in this "joyful exchange" am I turned from my faithless, loveless, hopeless self-absorption to a new ec-static or ec-centric existence that lives in joyful faith before God the heavenly Father and in Spirit-charged love for all in need. Sustained in Romans 8 hope for this groaning earth to which Christ will come for the "redemption of our bodies," believers look beyond the sufferings of this present time to the coming of the earth's merciful and eternal King at His parousia.

For this perseverance in hope, not least of Christ's gifts is His own messianic Spirit, who first led Him through the cross to the crown and who now makes believers *Christ*-ians—that is, Luther's "little Christs," priestly mediators of God's redeeming love to the world as they die to self to rise to newness of life. It should be firmly noted that the teaching of the priesthood of all believers does not mean the right to one's own private relation to God, nor the right to private interpretation of Scripture, nor does it reject the mediation of the Spirit and grace to believers by the external Word delivered by preachers and the evangelical sacraments of bath and meal. Luther does not mean that I am a priest for "me, myself, and I." He means that in Christ, with others in Christ, we become "little Christs" of God's mercies to and for others. And not just the clergy, the ordained "priests," but all the baptized are made such priests in Christ for others. The differentiation here is otherwise. The ordained have a specific ministry in the church *to* the Word and sacraments, to see to it that they are delivered to the joy and edification of Christ's holy people. But all of Christ's holy people, clergy too, have a ministry *from* the gospel Word and sacraments to the world in need. Clergy are such "lay" people too.

There is a trinitarian reciprocity at work here. The Son obtains us by His life's oblation; the Spirit brings us to fulfillment by preaching the Son to us, telling what He has done for us so that Christ begins to live in us. The persons of Christ the Son and the Holy Spirit, with their respective works, are distinguishable yet inseparable. Hence, where Christ is not preached, there is no Holy Spirit to sanctify by granting faith and newness of life. And where the Holy Spirit is not given, Christ remains a distant historical exemplar or a heavenly ideal with no power to draw near, to seek, to find, to embrace, and thus to change us. Moreover, there are many kinds of spirits, Luther notes, each with its own agenda. But only the Spirit of the Father and the Son—that is, the One who sanctifies believers by uniting them with Christ the Son to live before God the heavenly Father—is holy. Accordingly, *knowing* Christians are to *test* the spirits, to see whether they are of the one true God—the test being, according to 1 John

4:1–4, confession of the Spirit who led Jesus *in the flesh*, which has become the Spirit's *temple*.

The Holy Spirit therefore first leads us, Luther notes with emphasis, into His holy community, there to preach, offer, bestow, and apply Christ to us. The holy community is not the building but the unique people in the world, the "little flock" of the Good Shepherd, or, as I like to put it, the *Beloved Community*. As the Spirit gave Mary to conceive Christ, so the Spirit gives the ecclesia to be the "mother" of all believers, who conceives and bears every believer by the Word of God. Luther does not make conscious note of it, but his language here is precise and important. How does evangelization occur? As we saw in part 1, the Spirit brings neophytes into the Beloved Community, where they learn the good reasons for the love they experience there. One does not first convert someone who then affiliates with others to form a community of fellow-feeling or like-mindedness. Rather, the holy community is already there, for the preaching of the gospel precedes us individually and conforms us to its holy *tradition* (in the sense of 1 Cor. 15:1–11). Into this community the Spirit draws new-comers, who there learn Christ in the event of His joyful exchange. So they individually and personally come to faith and are born again *from above*, to be sure, but *into the ecclesia*—the "called out" earthly body of the risen Lord.

So Luther describes personal conversion not as a secret, inward, private event that then looks out to associate with the like-minded or like-feeling in a self-selected religious club. Rather, he thinks of the holy community of the Holy Spirit, the divinely given mediator who creates believers by the Word and sacraments, whose intimate struggle then is to learn to bear one another's burdens patiently. In this precise sense, Luther affirms that outside the ecclesia there is no salvation—that is, outside the external Word and its public commu-nity by which the Spirit works, there is no saving transformation of the human subject in conformity with Jesus Christ. But here believ-ers bear with one another, forgiving as they have been forgiven and so anticipating the fullness of human salvation in the coming of the Beloved Community of God.

Of course, this "exclusivity" of salvation in Christ's body raises for us today the acute problem of religious pluralism and public tolerance. Since for Luther faith must be free to be faith at all, we have a resource (endorsed by Rome for modern times in the Second Vatican Council's Decree on Religious Liberty, *Dignitatis Humanae*) for endorsing religious tolerance. Surely today we should be aiming at convergences rather than fueling now-habitual divergences. But we also have a mandate to be truthful about *differences*; genuine difference is the very presupposition of religious tolerance and the reason for the political need of it.

It is the willful ignorance of indifference to think that salvation is conceived identically in the world religions (or even conceived at all)—it is *not*. That is the very reason why the religions are different! It is simply analytically true, true "by definition," that there is no union with Christ for eternal life in the Trinity outside the ecclesia, which is its historical anticipation. It may be, if Christ descended into hell to proclaim liberty to its denizens, that the ecclesia is invisibly bigger than we can see. That is another question, which Luther probed but never resolved. With clarity of mind and forthright truthfulness, however, we can come in Luther's tradition of theology to a genuine knowledge of different "salvations" (including the peace of nonsalvation in versions of Buddhism) on offer in the religions of the world. That divergence is the real difference that divides religions as distinct communities in the world. On this level, what we can rather hope for politically is "achieving disagreement," in which hearing the other's critique conduces to one and all a humility before the one true God, who is not the captive idea of any religion, including the Christian religion.

And that brings us back to Luther. Luther stresses that the ecclesia actually has a peculiar, paradoxical righteousness. Its virtue is that sins are confessed rather than protested. Here mutual forbearance rather than self-righteous grandstanding prevails. The reason is that believers are still in process, *homo viator*, pilgrims trekking through the wilderness, on the way but not yet arrived. Their newness of life is only partial. For they are still organically connected by their participation in the common body to structures of malice and injustice that continue to infiltrate their newborn subjectivities and attempt to prevail over them. Thus, the battle of the Spirit against the flesh commences on baptism day, to conclude only on resurrection day. In the interim, life in the holy community within a world still structured by malice into systems of injustice is a matter of struggle and resistance that persists until all things are made new. To persevere in this struggle, the catechism next gives words from the Lord's own lips that daily implore the coming victory of God's reign.

8

The Christian Life

The New Obedience

One of the great strengths of evangelicalism is that its people—not just its preachers—know how to pray and are not shy to pray, out loud and in public. In this they are better imitators of Martin Luther's piety than are most Lutherans. As a lifelong Lutheran, let me begin with a confession. I could say, "I don't know how to pray." That would be true enough, and true to the topic before us, in which the Lord mercifully puts on our lips, as Luther emphasizes, the very words that teach us to pray. We learn to pray, if these words teach us, in union with the Son, hence to "our" heavenly Father, in the power of the Spirit, who bears witness that we are indeed the children of God. Tacitly, evangelicals know this and practice it far better than do traditional Lutherans. Why is that?

The confession I would make is that in spite of my being a lifelong Lutheran, this latter part of Luther's Large Catechism for many years made little sense to me. All of a sudden, it seemed to me, I was given a new list of divine commands to obey! Is the gospel nothing but a resource for renewed striving to fulfill the law? Or is it at bottom only a new law by virtue of new and improved commandments? I have come to realize that my incomprehension of Luther's exposition of prayer as the newness of life determined by the sacraments of incorporation (baptism) and sustenance (Lord's Supper) for pilgrim people not yet arrived (confession) is due to the way I was educated in seminary. I was led to the best and brightest lights in twentieth-century German Lutheranism. While Paul Tillich and Rudolph Bultmann became early favorites, my teachers at seminary directed us to Werner Elert, Gerhard Ebeling, and Paul Althaus. There are important differences between these theologians, but all had in common a strong law-gospel distinction—so strong that today I would call it a *dualism* that separates, rather than a *distinction* that clarifies, the elements of a dynamic unity according to the purpose clause of Paul, "God has imprisoned all in disobedience *so that* he may be merciful to all" (Rom. 11:32). As we have seen, this is Luther's distinction between the alien and the proper works of God, who kills in order to make alive.

What I got from my seminary education, however, was that the *pure* point of the gospel is to effect a liberating word that sets free from the law—as if the law, not our sin, which the law exposes and criticizes, were our true enemy. We were taught in seminary that "gospel-plussing"—that is, adding something further to the liberating word that sets free from the law—is the singular heresy. There are no commands any longer for the liberated person. For freedom Christ has set us free! Submitting to commands came at the cost of falling away from grace and squandering freedom.

Never mind that this counsel nullifies Luther's catechetical treatment of the Christian life in this final part of the Catechism! Never mind that Luther, an astute student of the apostle Paul, is following the latter's order of the indicative of grace preceding and grounding the imperative to live as children of the light—or as article 6 of the Augsburg Confession titled the matter, the "New Obedience"! Never mind that Luther reorganized the catechism to conclude with four mandates or imperative parts that we study in this chapter: the Lord's Prayer, baptism, the Lord's Supper, and confession. What these four parts have in common is, well, just what the radical Lutherans of the twentieth century feared: "gospel-plussing"—if by "gospel" we mean *only* the declaration of forgiveness by the imputation of the heavenly Judge and not also the gift of the Spirit for repentance and the new life of the just who live by faith.

Yet that would be not a pure gospel but a most truncated one, this so-called radical Lutheranism. What is really going on here is a reprise of the old doctrine of extrinsic righteousness and forensic imputation from Lutheran orthodoxy claiming to be a pure Luther theology. The limited validity of this old doctrine of forensic imputation is that of an abstraction that clarifies, so that the justified believer assuredly knows on every step of her pilgrim way, "Nothing in my hands I bring, solely to Thy cross I cling." But if faith, which knows just this, justifies, it is already that Spirit-wrought trust in the person of Christ that lays hold of His promise, "I am yours and you are mine." In that case of Spirit-bestowed justifying faith, which gives new birth to a believer, sanctification cannot in reality be extracted from justification and turned into a secondary and subsequent human response to a primary word of forgiveness. The wooden scheme of "imputed righteousness first, effective renewal following" turns a clarifying abstraction into a dualistic psychology. It turns a protest within Catholicism into a protest against Catholicism.

The clarity that can and should help the justified persevere in faith is the *propter Christum*—that is, Christian righteousness is "on account of Christ," not on account of the believer's works, thoughts, feelings, or progress. Affirming that truth of salvation by grace, not only at the beginning of Christian life but all the way to the end, is crucial to the perseverance of the saints in the face of the persistence of sin in the life of the redeemed. If Christians in fact regularly stumble and fall and remain entangled, consciously or not, in webs of malice and injustice that permeate this fallen creation, then they need ever to be consoled with the truth of Romans 5: that being justified by faith, not yet sight, and in hope, not yet in fullness of reality, they nonetheless have peace with God. Out of this present assurance and not from fear of an uncertain future, then, the concrete Christian life moves forward in grace, from grace to grace, in the new obedience that begins to fulfill the holy law of God. Those justified by faith, then, are to be continually exhorted in the manner of the gospel indicative to be on earth what they are in heaven—that is, to realize in their earthly lives what already they are in the judgment of God, which justifies *propter Christum.*

These four parts of Luther's catechism tell liberated Christians how to live in the pleasure of God, their heavenly Father. Indeed, they command the children of God to come forth as sons and daughters. They empower Christian life as a life of invited prayer, a life lived conscientiously in the presence of God (*coram Deo*, before God). This is a life that daily moves forward by returning to its foundation in baptism, nurtured along the way by the eucharistic meal and the mutual consolation and conversation of sisters and brothers, where they are free to confess sins rather than protest them. All these directives for new life Luther explicitly grounds in the creative, powerful "command of God."

Educated as I was, however, Luther's actual words about the "command of God" could only sound like a return to life under the law, as if we were now to prove how worthy of grace we were by praying, by observing sacraments with accompanying ritual, and by—heaven forbid!—revealing one's sin and brokenness to others. What I did not understand is that in Luther's theological reasoning, freedom is not only freedom from, say, guilt or punishment. True freedom is freedom for love, just as the apostle affirms at the end of Galatians in 5:13. Love is what Christians are freed for; these directives tell Christians what they *get* to do as those freed from both the guilt and the power of sin.

As we have seen to this point, then, Luther's catechism is structured by a sequence that passes from God the Creator's holy demand on His wayward creature to the same God's redeeming and sanctifying gifts of Himself in the missions of the Son and the Spirit. Thus now we proceed to the same God's renewed creative command, inviting creatures into creation's fulfillment: Implore the coming of God's reign! Commit your earthly cares to the fulfillment of this promise! Give yourself daily to death in Christ so that you are prepared to meet Him when he comes in glory! Keep struggling, hence suffering, faith alive by feeding on the Bread of life! Unburden yourself when you fail, as you surely will in the ebb and flow of apocalyptic battle, and hear the renewed word of forgiveness concretely spoken to you as often as needed by trusted and trustworthy sisters and brothers! By these exhortations, Luther says, God draws us to Himself in longing and in love. By obedience to these commands, the false desires of still-straying hearts are revealed, repented of, and patiently ordered anew to the one true God, who is alone worthy of all our fear, love, and trust.

The Lord's Prayer[1]

In this light, Luther says, it is a wicked and unfree heart that flees God and does not want to pray. On the one hand, in the religion business this heart can disguise itself by mumbling rote words or aimless sounds, or it can boldly and articulately bargain with God. But it can never simply receive a gift in joy and thanksgiving, nor implore gifts (as opposed to rewards) for those in need, beginning with its own broken self. On the other hand, if the believer is stuck in introspection, she will never be sure that she is pure enough to pray. The human heart, in its wayward and conflicting desires, is an abyss—a labyrinth, as Calvin put it.

But prayer is not based on the faltering and ambiguous desires of the conflicted saint who still struggles in the Spirit and against the flesh. Prayer and its personal and communal habits are *given* by the same Spirit as divine remedy to conflicted souls with ambiguous desires. Like doctor's orders, prayer is commanded for the healing of such struggling souls. "The command indicates the sickness for which faith is the medication, while Prayer shows from where this drug could be obtained (WA 7:204)."[2] Such prayer, commanded and provided, makes those who pray subagents of their own healing as the hearty "Amen" of faith is evoked, learned, and progressively internalized. We pray because God's creative command summons us, indeed effectively giving what it demands, putting even the very words of Jesus the Son on our lips and turning believers into warriors under Christ's saving lordship in apocalyptic battles against sin, death, and devil. Luther thus grasps the apocalyptic frame of reference in Jesus's kingdom prayer. To pray is to undertake battle. The believer gets to fight—not with a sword but with prayer—against the liar and murderer from the beginning.[3]

As divine command, the Lord's Prayer in its two parts corresponds to the Ten Commandments in its two tables. One could say that the Lord's Prayer is renewed torah, when we understand torah as divine instruction, not just commandments that are more precisely translated by the concept of the law. Christ, then, is the end of the law in the sense of the legal demand for righteousness through specified works. But Christ is the fulfillment of torah in the sense of effectively giving what God creatively commands. In this light, the first part of the Lord's Prayer, according to Luther, concerns the right ordering of the believer's relation to God, and the second part concerns right relations with creatures. Luther sees fulfillment of the first table of the law in the invocation of God as our heavenly Father through the Son, Jesus Christ, in that this One is the true God whom we can fear, love, and trust above all. This God is the God who purely gives, and in prayer we appropriate this giving as those gifted in God with all His treasures. His kingdom is pure gift, which comes without our prayer, but we pray in this prayer that it comes also to us, into us, making us over, taking us over. In just this way of prayerful receptivity, we become agents—*warriors* who do mighty battle, according to Luther, against the devil, the world, and flesh, not with swords of steel, but by learning through our own Gethsemanes the hearty "Amen" of the just who live by faith: "Thy will be done!"

Christ reigns in believers not least in delivering us from the false prophecies and deceptive promises of those pseudo-messiahs who use God's name falsely to deceive and lead astray.[4] But Christ also reigns by progressively taking hold of us. "God's word is holy when, wielded by the Holy Spirit, it does what it is supposed to do, taking hold of the heart."[5] *Fides ex corde*, faith from the heart, is the faith taught and learned in prayer. So we pray that we may remain true to the Word in living as children of the heavenly Father, freed from deception, freed for love, for in such lives God's name is hallowed rather than blasphemed. In this way true prayer progressively changes the consciousness of those who pray; even more deeply, it transforms the desires of the heart at their root.

Thus the petition for daily bread expands into awareness of all creation as God's gift, which makes for peace just as it protests against the oppression of the poor that works for war. The petition for forgiveness before God, coupled with mutual forgiveness on earth, is the sign that God's grace has changed the consciousness of those who pray, making them blessed peacemakers whose desire is no longer for war. The petitions for deliverance against the evil one and his wiles in turn preach back to God His own promises, summoning God to stir up His power and come to our aid in our need. In just this way, the gift of perseverance is imparted in the teeth of much adversity and opposition.

Baptism[6]

Baptism is the ceremonious public reception of the newcomer into the community of Christ. As with the Lord's Prayer, Luther stresses that baptism is God's word, neither law nor promise but gospel imperative, the new creative command. Thus it is not a self-invented rite or religious practice but was revealed from above on the banks of the river Jordan when the Lord emerged from the waters. The theophany there of the Father above speaking over His beloved Son, on whom He sent His Spirit for battle with the unholy spirits, inaugurates the reign of God. With Jesus's Easter victory, His baptism is henceforth performed in the Triune name to "snatch" believers from the "jaws of hell" and deliver them safely into the kingdom of Christ. Baptism thus comes to us as the front line of the reign of God; it happens to us in the form of being put to death with Christ and in Him rising to newness of life. It is a specific form with a specific function of God's "external" word that comes to the self from outside the self to transform the self by uniting us with Christ and endowing us with His Spirit.

Luther's polemic is aimed, accordingly, against the new "sects" and "sectarians" who reject sacramental baptism as being an "external thing," a mere ceremony that washes the body but cannot reach and touch the desires of the heart. Luther, however, surely agrees with these critics that the "heart" is the place in the world where the change of regeneration has to occur, if a child of fallen humanity is to be truly converted—that is, *ex corde*—from the seat of her desires into a Christian. The Spirit imparts *fides ex corde*, faith from the heart, faith that transforms desire by refocusing it on the one true God, the only eternal good. The baptized, consequently, seek first the kingdom of God and its righteousness. They pray to their heavenly Father, "Thy kingdom come! Thy will be done!" They learn to have no other gods. So at its best, the dispute here between Luther, with his faith in the water ceremony as the Spirit's visible word, and adherents of "believer's baptism" is a family quarrel. Both agree that faith that justifies is *fides ex corde*; the dispute revolves around the questions of whether and how the Spirit bestows faith in baptism.

To illustrate this penetration from the outside into the heart of human desire, Luther employs some images that can become misleading if taken too far. One that became famous (if not notorious) in the nineteenth century was the image of the kernel and the husk, as if the exterior wrapper, the husk, could be removed and discarded in order to get at the nutmeat. But Luther's point is that God hides Himself in His revelation, in bread and wine and water as also words of human preachers, just as in the humanity of Jesus Christ. God hides Himself in this way to approach humanity body-to-body, embodied, to "be there for us" as we in space and time are *there* for one another, somewhere *in particular*. So this water, not any water, becomes the bath of God. This bread, not any bread, becomes the body of Christ. This prayer, not any prayer, is the Lord's Prayer. Hence for Luther, the kernel and the husk cannot be separated; they come together as a package deal, where and when the Spirit pleases to evoke and sustain faith.

Indeed, Luther says this water has become an "eternal water" by virtue of its sacramental union with the living and eternal Word of God, the Second Person of the Trinity, incarnate for us as the Lamb who was slain. Thus this sacramental water for spiritual drowning is capable of being grasped by the senses as something that comes from outside the self, available not to introspection but rather, once again, to "extraspection." Faith depends on this objectivity that the Word acquires in the bath, which addresses its promise to the baptized personally: you who here die with Christ will likewise rise with Him. Thus the certainty of faith rests on a historical event: *Baptizatus sum*, "I am baptized!"—in other words, obtained, won, claimed by Christ and sealed by His Spirit, dead to sin but alive to God.

Yet this objectivity of baptism as the foundation of the Christian life remains a matter of faith, not sight. What is objective is the fact of my baptism; what is faith in this matter is in the event of God's claim. We thus come to the difficult idea of Luther's theology of the cross: that God hides precisely in His revelation, so also in His sacraments. That God hides in this way to gain us body-to-soul has for Luther two implications. First, faith must have an object to which to cling. Second, faith remains faith, not sight, in just this reliance on an external object in the world that promises extraordinary things.

To say that I am elect or chosen may be true, but it has no objective form like saying, "I am baptized." In the latter case, something happened visibly, something tangibly occurred in the world. This something that was done is now a fact that cannot be undone. It bears facticity. So also the fact that this immersion in water was done at the command and in the name of the Triune God. As such, baptism is divinely commanded to effect deliverance from sin, death, and the devil. It is the bath of regeneration that does what it says and says what it does.

Luther stresses this performative nature of the regenerating word, "I baptize you in the Name . . . ," against the "sectarians" who have turned Luther's own teaching of "faith alone" against the external and visible word of the sacraments rather than against the idolatry of works in the human heart, as Luther intended. The false application of the kernel-and-husk image in the nineteenth century had its precedent in those contemporaries of Luther who regarded him as still half-mired in papist error for retaining sacraments as an external prop over against a purely mental word taken by faith alone. In my ancestral land of Slovakia during the nineteenth century, for example, some au courant Lutheran pastors would baptize by dipping their thumb in water and making a damp sign of the cross on the infant's forehead. In this way they dramatized their anti-Catholic point that it is the word *alone* that effects anything, that the water is a next-to-incidental addition to the word.

Luther hardly thinks this way. Careful reading of his exposition in this part of the Large Catechism shows that the sign of water for him is *immersion. Drowning* the old Adam/Eve, as Romans 6 teaches, is the very thing signified in the sacramental action or visible word, which is the specific form that the gospel command takes in inaugurating anyone into the battle of the reign of God. What does that say about contemporary practices of sprinkling? Luther quotes Augustine's dictum that the word is added to the element and thus a sacrament is made. Surely, sprinkling and dipping are "valid" applications of an element, water, if we want to get legalistic about it. But do they properly signify what immersion (dunking) signifies—namely, death, drowning, being crucified with Christ? Or do we shy away from even wishing to signify that? In fact, have not evangelicals who "dunk" better preserved in this regard Luther's insight into Paul's teaching in Romans 6 than "sprinkling" Lutherans?

Luther added an excursus on the practice of baptizing infants. The basic thought here is the old dictum *Abusus non tollit usum* (Abuse does not disqualify right use). But what is right use? Let us note well: Luther concedes that baptism is abused in the indiscriminate, not to say promiscuous, baptism of infants who are presented for the sacrament for the wrong reasons or motives.[7] Why else would he innovate in the catechetical tradition by adding a section on baptism, if not to instruct and thus properly prepare? It would be a great advance for us today if we could come even this far to acknowledge that baptism is as abused in the indiscriminate practice common among all who baptize infants as it is by those who rebaptize. Pastors who baptize infants of parents without taking the time and the care to instruct them in what they are doing, in the hope of "drawing them in," are not evangelizing but trafficking with the Word of God.

In his own day, Luther justified infant baptism because the Holy Spirit had confirmed this practice for a thousand years by making Christians out of these baptized infants. In this way Luther once again indicates that he does not understand himself to be rejecting Catholicism but rather reforming it. Even more central to his theology, however, is the thought that faith does not create baptism but receives it. Baptism creates and forms faith, which makes perfect gospel sense if baptism is identified not as the water rite as such but with the spiritual reality it signifies, dying with Christ to sin in order to rise to newness of life. Thus, even if an unbaptized adult comes to faith, the faith to which this person comes is faith ordered to baptism—that is, to the public act of reception into the ecclesia by the water ceremony signifying death and new life.

Because this is what baptism properly signifies, Luther rightly infers, rebaptizing is not permitted inasmuch as it effectively declares the prior baptism false, along with the ministry that performed it and the church that sponsors it. Rebaptism is thus a schismatic act. I would go so far as to suggest that Luther would have tolerated a normal practice of adult baptism, provided there was no rebaptism. But in his time the two notions of restricting baptism to adults and rebaptism (of those "falsely" baptized as infants) were tied together in a single knot. Positively expressed, Luther's view was that the church as a community brings the child to the watery grave in the trust that the Spirit will work faith, and so we are to preach and teach the child about her baptism so that the Spirit works through this word of personal address. In this way we retain the substance, the treasure, the kernel in the husk.

Luther concludes his defense of infant baptism by considering some objections. Daily return to baptism is precisely how real progress in the Christian life occurs. Luther expects growth in the Christian virtues of faith, hope, and love throughout life. So what if the old creature predominates and this progress does not occur or is not visible? That may mean several things: the battle is fierce (trench warfare, not blitzkrieg), or baptism is being resisted, or we do not see all that is going on. Thus the mutual consolation and conversation of the

sisters and brothers is needed. A good pastor or fellow Christians
will discern and counsel wisely. They will not judge superficially by
appearances but speak to the heart. They will call out resistance,
noting that the power to repent of one's resistance to baptism, moreover, is nothing but return to baptism. For baptism is not only the
Spirit's announcement of one's new identity in Christ but also the
Spirit's endowment of power to live this way with gifts for enriching
the community of Christ.

Baptism remains forever; it is the rock of personal certitude in faith.
The idea that baptism is good only for remitting the sins committed
up to that point in life, going back to Jerome's theology, makes baptism next to useless for life after post-baptismal sin. Baptism being
made useless by post-baptismal sin, Jerome had to invent another
sacrament, penance, as the emergency lifeboat available after the
wreck of the good ship *Baptism*. From this, all the "slaughter of
conscience" that followed was mandatory confession and prescribed
works of penance—for Luther, a pastoral disaster. But the entire life
of the believer is one of repentance, turning to the returning Lord,
a turning that begins with and ever returns to sacramental baptism
until the sign is fulfilled in the resurrection of the body.

The Lord's Supper[8]

The Lord's Supper is the sacrament of reunion with the community of
Christ: the believers dispersed into the world reassemble as the body of
Christ (1 Cor. 11:18) to partake of the body of Christ in anticipation
of His public manifestation to all (11:26). In keeping with this teaching
of Paul in 1 Corinthians, Luther accordingly affirms something more
concrete than an evanescent "real presence." Presence means *being
there*, somewhere in time and place. What kind of presence can there
be other than a "real" one? Luther affirms this *reality* of Christ being
there for us as promised, as the One who is and remains forever the
body born of Mary and crucified under Pontius Pilate. He affirms
Christ's *bodily* presence. The Sacrament of the Altar is "the true body
and blood, in and under bread and wine, for us to eat and drink."

Yet this bodily presence is not a "Capernaum" presence, "like sausage hanging in the butcher shop" (see John 6:59–60). To talk about this paradoxical presence of Christ "born of the Virgin Mary and crucified under Pontius Pilate yet raised on the third day" before His public parousia at the end of days, Luther thinks with Paul, who can distinguish the glorified body of the risen Lord from flesh and blood, which cannot inherit the kingdom of God (1 Cor. 15:42–50). From this Pauline perspective, he can also accommodate the Johannine teaching that the "flesh" of Christ is food, indeed the living bread that comes down from heaven, since John 6 also rejects that "carnal" understanding of the "flesh" imagined by disciples from Capernaum who took offense and deserted Jesus at the "hard saying" about eating His "flesh" for salvation. Terminological or semantic differences should not obscure the unity of witness between John 6 and 1 Corinthians to the paradoxical presence of the very One who suckled at Mary's breast and died impaled on the Roman stake, in His new body risen and glorified, not to be absent but to be present to recapitulate (literally, to "re-head") His own, who by eating His body become His body.

It is likely that the apostolic father Ignatius of Antioch, when he wrote to the Smyrnaeans around 110, had in mind this schism in John 6 when the disciples from Capernaum deserted Jesus at his "hard saying":

> Now note well those who hold heretical opinions about the grace of Jesus Christ that came to us; note how contrary they are to the mind of God. They have no concern for love, none for the widow, none for the orphan, none for the oppressed, none for the prisoner or the one released, none for the hungry or thirsty. They abstain from Eucharist and prayer because they refuse to acknowledge that the Eucharist is the flesh of our savior Jesus Christ, which suffered for our sins and which the Father by his goodness raised up.[9]

While it is unlikely that Luther knew this text, he would have loved it. For Luther too, unlike ordinary bread that we consume, metabolize, and thus change into ourselves, this heavenly food changes us into

it. The anti-docetic stress on the personal identity of the risen, glori-
fied, and paradoxically present Christ, moreover, is at the heart of
Luther's *Christus pro nobis*, Christ for us, the only saving Christ—as
Ignatius also witnesses.

As with the Lord's Prayer and baptism, so also the Lord's Supper
is grounded in the creative divine command "Do this," meaning not
"Do this whenever you happen to think about having Communion"
but rather "This is how I want to be remembered, as the One who
laid down His body and blood for you, once on Calvary, but also now
whenever you assemble as my body in the world." The creative divine
command is, as we say today, *performative*. It is a performance, a
speech act that says what it gives and gives what it says, though only
faith benefits from this performance of God's creative word. In the
words of institution faithfully spoken by the presiding minister, Christ
Himself not only speaks but also effects what is said, so that of all the
bread in the world, this particular bread is singled out (consecrated,
sanctified) as the place of His body given for you, with this particular
cup of blessing, the cup of His blood, shed for you.

If this faith-nurturing word of Christ, who presents and imparts
Himself today as the One who once for all suffered in His own body
and died, is truly what the sacrament is, then the question of how it
benefits the believer almost answers itself. Christ does not so much
offer benefits as He offers Himself. The gift of Christ's innocent self-
offering for us, the guilty, secures and vouchsafes the forgiveness of
real, not fictitious, sinners. Here the barrier between the holy God and
sinful humanity is breached by the interposition of Christ's body on
the cross, so that sin disappears into forgiveness and all the treasures
of God come gushing forth for life and salvation.

As with prayer and baptism, the divine gifts do not depend on faith
but are given for the sake of faith, so that God who gives can take hold
of consciousness and organize anew the desires of the heart. So the
newborn creature of God is fed and fit for renewed battle against the
sinful self, the hostile world, and the uncanny devil and is expected to
progress forward in faith, hope, and love. Faith is the understanding
appropriation of what is offered *pro me*, "for me," making it my

very own in the way one takes into possession a gift as opposed to a reward. Following Paul, however, Luther sees that unfaithful and ignorant reception is possible—and scandalously so. Such eating and drinking despises the body of Christ in that it "show[s] contempt for the church of God and humiliates those who have nothing" (1 Cor. 11:22). The cup of blessing thus can become a cup of poison when it is not received faithfully and for the purpose intended, as known by discernment and self-examination (1 Cor. 11:29–30).

Note well: in this case the Lord's Supper is not a nothing, an empty and inefficacious sign, but a poison, the thing signified working as a curse and not the divinely intended blessing. The reason is that the dear cost of the crucified and risen body of Christ for the holy communion of redeemed sinners is blasphemed by undiscerning, worldly partisanship (1 Cor. 11:18). In principle, the Lord's Supper is meant for the evangelized, catechized, and baptized people of God, who in faith know what they are doing when by eating and drinking they are being turned into the body of Christ.

Luther attends as well to the much-botched question about the frequency of Communion. I say "botched" because the actual history in the West of how often a Christian should receive goes something like this. When the European peoples were converted to Christianity en masse by the conversion of their warlords, the illiterate and un-catechized multitudes brought with them all sorts of superstitions. Stealing the consecrated bread for magical use as a talisman was commonplace. Spilling from the chalice or guzzling the wine took place too. After the cup was removed from the laity on the grounds that body and blood are interchangeable "elements," so that Christ was said to be equally present in either, and after Communion wafers were invented so that they would dissolve when placed upon the outstretched tongue (making it difficult to take the bread home for magical purposes), the question of whether it was necessary to commune at all inevitably arose.

The ruling was that, if one was to be counted a Christian, it was necessary to commune at least once a year, after private confession and during Holy Week. The celebration of the Eucharist on Sunday had largely become a spectator sport. The chief thing was witnessing the "hocus-pocus" of the transubstantiation, the priest sacrificing the body of Christ to appease an angry God on behalf of the sinful masses gathered to witness the offering. "Hocus-pocus" is a corruption of the Latin *Hoc est corpus meum*, "This is my body." This was the "botched" practice Luther inherited. While he refused to make a law about frequency of Communion, he emphatically taught that Communion is the gift of God for Christians in the struggle of the Spirit against the flesh, and so he fervently exhorted that the gift be taken seriously and received gratefully. Yet it cannot be said that a full recovery of the patristic practice was achieved by Luther's reforms.

He was so concerned with evangelizing and catechizing the common people that the church services practically turned into academic lectures. The vestments of the learned doctor replaced the regalia of the priesthood. Luther had advised reception of Communion at least four times a year, under his historical circumstances a fourfold increase in frequency. But this intended increase turned into a de facto limit. To this day in Europe, quarterly Communion is the prevailing practice, offered for those who desire it after the congregation is dismissed from the preaching service. Even in professedly Lutheran churches, Communion is not especially understood as the gospel word of God, "This is my body, given for you," offered then as the particular way in which Christ commands that He be remembered among His faithful. Only in recent years, thanks to the liturgical movement, has Communion been restored as belonging to the normal shape of Christian assembly. But, one fears, this renewal has more to do with belonging than believing, aesthetics instead of dogmatics.

For the historical Luther, it is the devil who hates Holy Communion and so mocks mere bread and wine on the altar as nothing but bread and wine, just as he mocks the water of baptism as mere water, the external word of preachers as mere opinion, and the human Jesus, born of Mary and suffered under Pontius Pilate, as nothing but another fool for God, denied, betrayed, abandoned, and defeated once and for all. According to Luther, the devil deceives by making such appearances seem to be the whole story and the end of the story.

Jesus Christ—empty idol or icon of the living God? In either case, we deal with the same appearance (*persona*) in the world, just as the word "This is my body" asserts. "Take away such assertions," Luther asserted against Erasmus, and "you take away Christianity!"

Confession[10]

Confession is not a sacrament as such but a sacramental practice that negotiates between baptism into Christ and reception of His Supper. It consists in contrite confession of sin and pronunciation of divine forgiveness. It may be public and general, as is customary in many Lutheran churches. It may also be private and particular, a typical form of pastoral counseling. The later Luther not only allows but also emphatically endorses confession; indeed, he exhorts Christians to it in this concluding part of his Large Catechism. As we have seen, Luther refused to make a legalistic rule about the frequency of Communion, as had been done previously, since confession to the priest had been made a precondition to worthy reception and was extorted with a checklist of prohibited thoughts, words, and deeds. This legalistic practice, according to Luther, was a form of clerical tyranny based on coercion and fear, a voyeuristic act of torture demanding an enumeration of embarrassing sins, producing a "slaughter of souls or consciences."

Yet Luther's critique was intended not to remove confession but to purify it. It does not mean that Luther drops the "precondition" of penitent self-examination, if one wants to put it that way; confession remains for him the needed preparation of the baptized people of God for worthy reception that will prove to be comfort to their souls, not poison. As in the previous part on the Sacrament of the Altar, Luther declared on behalf of the Reformation churches, "We do not intend to admit to the sacrament and administer it to those who do not know what they seek or why they come," so here also he writes, "Anyone who will not believe the gospel, live according to it, and do what a Christian ought to do should enjoy none of its benefits."

Is this legalism? Does it mean we have to do something to be worthy of grace? An antinomian doctrine of justification would suggest that Luther here betrays the basic Reformation insight into grace. But Luther won't cooperate with an antinomian doctrine of justification. His law is God's law, and its sacred work is the daily crucifixion of the old Adam. He writes that those who in principle eschew this practice of baptism in confession and are repulsed at the very thought of the Spirit's struggle against sin in their lives should rather draw the conclusion "I am not a Christian."

For Luther, such folks should hardly be hoodwinked into taking Communion without understanding how in reality they therewith take upon themselves the cross of Jesus so that the Spirit can do battle against their flesh. Grace is not unconditional acceptance but the extraordinary favor and good pleasure of the Father that rests on the Son and is now bestowed on those who are in Christ by the Spirit's work of killing to make alive. It is therefore God's costly way, by the cross of Jesus, to reconcile His enemy. Where this Romans 6 struggle of the Spirit against the flesh is unknown, there is no Christian life. Invoking a blanket amnesty in the name of grace turns Christ into nothing but a supposed revelation or illustration of a universal truth of divine permissiveness; it makes the work of the Holy Spirit in forming Christians into holy people pointless since it has simply abandoned holiness altogether. Abandoning holiness is a cipher for the abandonment of the one true God.

In other words, baptism is the radical hospitality of the holy God, and confession is practice in personally and concretely appropriating this extraordinary favor of the righteous for the unrighteous. This gift is not legalistically preconditioned on our doing something, but rather consists of the work in us of the Spirit given to us, which manifests in repentance and faith. Thus, those who approach the altar seek the body of the Lord, who was crucified and raised for them, so that they may be renewed in this Lord's forgiving love and thus enjoy His life and salvation in newness of life.

Reception that is unconscious, rote, and conformist, though allegedly unconditional, is motivated only by a desire to belong, not to believe. It is so cheap that you can hardly give it away. At least medieval Catholics thought grace was something precious enough to work for! How much more cheapened can grace be made by Protestants? But a properly *catechized* Christian—remember, we are drawing now to the conclusion of the Large *Catechism*—is one who is coming to live *consciously*, hence also *conscientiously*, before God, made all the more aware of sin by the *holying* Spirit, all the more in need of grace as forgiveness, all the more engaged in his or her own personal struggle to progress forward in faith, hope, and love. Luther can hardly contain his disgust at the "cheap grace" that "quickly understands whatever gives us an advantage and grasps with uncommon ease whatever in the gospel is mild and gentle." He continues, "But such pigs, as I have said, should not have the gospel or any part of it."

The Christian's work as a newborn child of God is to know sin, to lament it (contrition), to desire the consolation of forgiveness assured, and on this basis to renew in the struggle of the Christian life. The Spirit's work is to provide, through the minister's words *Ego te absolvo*, "I absolve you," that bone-deep assurance of God's mercy coming from outside the self but going all the way down to the marrow of the soul. In this concrete and personal word of grace, the Spirit is present powerfully to raise the believer again to the lifelong battle against the flesh. Such confession is precisely not a "magnificent work" of self-torture to present to God as a bribe, as if God's love for us increased the more we hated ourselves. It is rather a heavenly virtue, an act of verbalizing and unburdening ourselves of the weight of guilt that actually weighs us down and paralyzes us. "For Christ bears all sin, if only it displeases us, so that our sins become Christ's and His righteousness ours"—this joyful exchange, we have learned, is the leitmotif of Luther's theology. Confession *is* this joyful exchange from the human side, where the human side is decided by the holying Spirit. At the heart of confession, joyful exchange is thus practiced. Knowing this, the well-catechized believer grounded in the daily practice of baptism is moved by conscience to free and willing confession as a sick person is moved by accurate diagnosis to medicine that cures disease and soothes its pain.

We should carefully note how much Luther talks in this section about the *desires of the heart*. It is not beliefs held in the mind that justify, even the belief that God is loving, kind, gentle, forgiving, and so on. Such beliefs may be true, but until by the work of the Spirit they crucify the wayward desires of the old Adam's heart and teach the children of Adam to seek first the kingdom of God and its righteousness, they are clanging gongs and empty symbols. By confession, our seeking—that is, our desire—is reordered by the first commandment and fulfilled in us, works in progress that we are, by the Son and His Spirit.

Postlude

W E HAVE LEARNED FROM LUTHER in this study that the ecclesia is to be a disciplined community of belief holding to the confession of Jesus Christ and the Triune God with all that this implies; in just this way it *resists* (recall the overture to this book on "A Mighty Fortress Is Our God") the powerful claims of this dying epoch until the kingdom of God comes. Luther's embattled ecclesiology is not only reflected in the trinitarian structure of his sober hymn "Lord, Keep Us Steadfast in Your Word,"[1] with three stanzas addressed successively to the Father, the Son, and the Holy Spirit. It is also evident in the hymn's petition for protection: "Support us in our final strife / and lead us out of death to life." In this interregnum, the church prays a protest: *O Lord, stop the murder!* We see in this hymn, then, Luther's theology of the nonviolent witness of the community of the martyrs, whose power in this world displays in *resistance*, whose steadfast, urgent, and repeated prayer and public witness is *Stop the murder!*

In the original text composed by Luther late in life, around 1542, the opening line reads somewhat scandalously to contemporary ears: "Lord, keep us steadfast in your Word and stop the murder by Pope and Turk, who want to thrust Jesus Christ your Son from your throne" (my translation). The sanitized text we have in the current hymnals substitutes something like "those who by deceit or sword" for the specific names "Pope and Turk." Such sanitizing edits have a long precedence; similar mitigations of Luther's pointed polemic can be traced all the way back to early Lutheranism. Admittedly, this editing is necessary in contemporary appropriation—appropriation that really makes a gift one's own and also inevitably transforms the gift into one's own life's resource. The only requirement here is intellectual honesty about what is received, what is left behind, and what is the transformed result. The editing of Luther's hymn text, then, is an example of the way in which the historical Luther's witness needs to be filtered from its original context if later generations in new situations are to appropriate the underlying theology. That underlying theology is found in the hymn's fervent prayer of protest, echoing the saints in heaven, according to the book of Revelation: *Stop the murder!*

As mentioned, we must know what we are doing in such modernizing of Luther's text. There is a fine line between honestly appropriating the theological legacy from the past and dishonestly claiming its prestige and authority while emptying the theology of its particular content. We learn to make this fine distinction by seeing just how timely and concrete Luther's text was in its own day and age. Perhaps surprisingly, what we won't understand correctly, if we don't pay careful attention to the change in our historical contexts, is the fundamentally *pacifist* stance that Luther articulated *christologically*.

This ethical implication of Luther's theology has been obscured by his panicked reaction to the Peasants' Revolt, when he urged its violent suppression. This lamentable overreaction, along with Thomas Müntzer's characterization of Luther as a "lackey of the princes," was taken up by Friedrich Engels and thence passed into the standard repertoire of Marxist tropes until it became a modern commonplace. Luther, in any case, is not being recommended in this study as a hero (or rejected as a villain) one way or another. What recommends Luther is his understanding and teaching of the Christian faith, which is distinguishable from his own performance as a Christian. And the salient point in this regard is recognition of the Christian's pacifism that Luther derives from his dogmatics, which to be sure he qualifies with his notion of the strange or alien work of divine love operative in God's "left-hand" kingdom of holy secularity.[2]

In the *Explanations of the Ninety-Five Theses* (1519), Luther had written that whoever resists the Turk resists God, for the Turk is God's rod to punish us wicked Christians for our sins[3]—a provocative thought also today for post-9/11 Americans. In Luther's time, the "Turks" were the powerful force of Islam conquering the Balkans and the Hungarian Empire and advancing into the heart of Europe. Thus, a decade after the Ninety-Five Theses, as the Turks were laying siege to Vienna and the emperor and the pope were calling for European religious unity in holy war against the invaders, Luther made the "two-kingdoms" clarification of this provocative claim.

What he was rejecting, he explained, is the false theology of the "holy crusade," as if Europeans made up an "army of Christians" undertaking holy war against Muslims. But Christians as Christians fight only with the Word and Spirit. It is the secular state that is responsible to God for the military defense of its people from aggression. The emperor may justifiably defend his people and property against the invading Turks, but not in the name of Christ. He must be satisfied with defense in the name of the people whom he is bound before God to serve. As Luther put it in his treatise *On War against the Turks* (1529),[4] Christians may fight in just wars under the emperor's banner, for soldiering is the preeminent instance of love's strange duty that sacrificially puts one's body between the aggressor and the intended victim. Yet as Christians they must determine conscientiously and before God whether a war is justified as a defensive action. If not, it is at peril of their salvation if they dare to participate in an unjust war. In this way, Luther sought to dismantle the theology of the holy crusade and ethically delimit warfare to the defensive tasks of the secular state.

Needless to say, Luther's dialectical combination of christological pacifism and political realism has had a mixed reception in Christian history. Perhaps the most penetrating critique of it is that every aggressor regards his aggression as justified; the best defense, as they say, is a good offense. In our times, so-called preventive war expressly chafes at the traditional limitation of just war to defensive warfare conducted by limited means. Moreover, with technology on the one side and massive global injustices on the other, warfare is evolving into forms unanticipated by traditional just-war ethics. This set of problems is one with which a man of the sixteenth century cannot much help us.

What can help us is a new appreciation of the seriousness of Luther's reading of the Sermon on the Mount—not the jaundiced view taken by Ernst Troeltsch and popularized in the United States by the Niebuhrs. Luther's christological "pacifism" consequently comes as something of a surprise, since his well-known (but not well-understood) doctrine of the two kingdoms allows resort to the secular sword for the defense of innocents against aggression, as we have just seen.[5] Luther encourages Christians to participate in this "police work" of the state to preserve a minimum of order in a fallen world. In distinction from that, however, Luther emphatically teaches that in the spiritual kingdom of Christ we have only the weapons of the Spirit. Fundamentally, the Spirit gives the power, not to slay the enemies of the state or even the church, but rather to stand with Christ the Crucified and confess Him alone as Lord of lords. This brave and defenseless witness is the one and only way to remain steadfast in God's word, when that word is not understood as some revealed worldview but as the holy judgment of God on the crucified Jesus spoken on Easter morn.

As the editor of *Luther's Works* further explains to us,[6] at the time of this hymn's composition the Holy Roman Empire had experienced terrible military defeats before the advancing Ottoman Turks. At the same time and for the sake of unity against the Turks, many princes were allying with the papacy in threatening to exterminate the Reformation by military force, while the wily king of France, pretending to be a protector of the papal church, even maneuvered to ally with the Turks against the empire! It was amid all these violent machinations of "wars and rumors of wars" that Luther had his people pray that God would stop the murder, even as he steeled the same people to face the murderers as martyrs rather than to deny Jesus Christ.

To this day, the Roman Catholic Church has not sufficiently or explicitly repented of its resort to violence to suppress the Reformation, beginning with its rush to judgment in the excommunication of Luther.[7] It is a matter of historical precision and of no little importance to note, however, that Luther's opponent was never the Catholic Church or even the bishop or church of Rome, but what in the early years he called "the papal party" and in the later years "the papacy." These were the "innovators" who had departed from the faith once delivered to the saints, a faith that the patristic church faithfully kept in adhering to "Jesus Christ, true God, begotten of the Father in eternity, and also a true human being, born of the Virgin Mary, . . . my Lord." So, as we have seen, in the Large Catechism Luther owned, passed on, and explained the inherited christological dogma from the Catholic tradition, which he understood in the same patristic way as a theology of the martyrs. In affirming patristic theology, Luther went so far as to claim that wherever this article concerning Jesus Christ had been maintained, there the true church had persisted—even without the clear articulation of the Reformation doctrine of justification!

Interestingly in this connection, this christological truth of the Catholic tradition is the very reason why Luther came to regard the innovation of the papacy as the antichrist. He held that according to 2 Thessalonians 2:4, the antichrist could *only* take up his seat "in the temple of God"—that is, in the *true* church. The papacy is the antichrist, not simply in opposing the Reformation, but first of all in oppressing the Christian community that remains under its own jurisdiction!

We are today rightly sensitized to the problems of demonizing rhetoric, and we realize that verbal violence is violence and not a spiritual alternative to it (as Luther rationalized his own violent polemics). Granting that, let us also recognize Luther's theological achievement in praying for peace, in imploring heaven to stop the murder, in preparing Christians for the nonviolent witness of martyrdom. He indeed saw and experienced real malice. That was no fantasy or superstition. He lived the last quarter century of his life as a condemned man, and that undoubtedly brutalized his consciousness, something expressed in his polemical outbursts against real and perceived foes, up to and including the now-notorious late-in-life attack on the Jews.

But the theologically salient conclusion to draw from this is that Luther sinned in returning evil for evil as he slipped into violent rhetoric. Having acknowledged that, as we must, we should also see that Luther's otherwise consistent teaching was peace, and peace with justice by the nonviolent way of prayer, witness, and even civil disobedience. That commitment is exactly why the hymn urgently prays for God's supervening protection and support. We can and should take this from Luther's teaching. *Stop the murder!* That is the embattled church's *ora et labora* (prayer and labor) until the final victory on this earth of the Beloved Community of God. *O Lord, stop the murder!*

As evangelicals in Euro-America reckon more and more with the reality of post-Christendom, meaning that Christendom's "revival" is no longer possible or even desirable, they will search for better ways to go forward, including the retrieval of the ancient way of the martyrs.[8] It is in this connection that Luther will be a valuable resource for them, both in preserving their precious teaching of the new birth and in decoupling it from debilitating habits of thought.

Appendix

Lyrics from the Hymns of Luther Discussed in This Book

Note: Luther's hymns are listed here in the order in which they are discussed in the book.

"A Mighty Fortress Is Our God"[1]

> 1 A mighty fortress is our God,
> a bulwark never failing;
> our helper he, amid the flood
> of mortal ills prevailing.
> For still our ancient foe
> doth seek to work us woe;
> his craft and power are great,
> and armed with cruel hate,
> on earth is not his equal.
>
> 2 Did we in our own strength confide,
> our striving would be losing,

1. Translation by Frederic Henry Hedge (public domain).

were not the right Man on our side,
the Man of God's own choosing.
Dost ask who that may be?
Christ Jesus, it is he;
Lord Sabaoth his name,
from age to age the same;
and he must win the battle.

3 And though this world, with devils filled,
should threaten to undo us,
we will not fear, for God has willed
his truth to triumph through us.
The prince of darkness grim,
we tremble not for him;
his rage we can endure,
for lo! his doom is sure;
one little word shall fell him.

4 That Word above all earthly powers
no thanks to them abideth;
the Spirit and the gifts are ours
through him who with us sideth.
Let goods and kindred go,
this mortal life also;
the body they may kill:
God's truth abideth still;
his kingdom is forever!

"To Jordan Came the Christ Our Lord"[2]

1 To Jordan came our Lord, the Christ,
To do God's pleasure willing,
And there was by St. John baptized,
All righteousness fulfilling;
There did He consecrate a bath
To wash away transgression,

2. Translation by Richard Massie (public domain).

And quench the bitterness of death
By His own blood and passion,
He would a new life give us.

2 So hear ye all, and well perceive
What God doth call a Baptism,
And what a Christian should believe
Who error shuns and schism:
That we should water use, the Lord
Declareth it His pleasure,
Not simple water, but the Word
And Spirit without measure;—
He is the true Baptizer.

3 To show us this He hath His word
With signs and symbols given;
On Jordan's banks was plainly heard
The Father's voice from heaven:
"This is My well-beloved Son,
In whom My soul delighteth;
Hear Him!" Yea, hear Him, every one,
When He Himself inviteth;
Hear and obey His teaching!

4 In tender manhood Jesus straight
To holy Jordan wendeth;
The Holy Ghost from heaven's throne
In dove-like form descendeth;
That thus the truth be not denied,
Nor should our faith e'er waver,
That the Three Persons all preside,
At Baptism's holy laver,
And dwell with the believer.

5 Thus Jesus His disciples sent
Go, teach ye every nation,
That, lost in sin, they must repent,
And flee from condemnation;
He that believes and is baptized

Obtains a mighty blessing,
A new-born man, no more he dies,
Eternal life possessing,
A joyful heir of heaven.

6 Who in this mercy hath not faith
Nor aught therein discerneth,
Is yet in sin, condemned to death
And fire that ever burneth;
His holiness avails him not,
Nor aught which he is doing;
His birth-sin brings all to naught,
And maketh sure his ruin;
Himself he cannot succor.

7 The eye of sense alone is dim,
And nothing sees but water;
Faith sees Christ Jesus, and in Him
The Lamb ordained for slaughter;
With the dear blood of Jesus,
Which from the sins, inherited
From fallen Adam, frees us,
And those we have committed.

"From Heaven Above to Earth I Come"[3]

1 From heaven above to earth I come
To bear good news to every home;
Glad tidings of great joy I bring,
Whereof I now will say and sing.

2 To you this night is born a Child
Of Mary, chosen virgin mild;
This little child, of lowly birth,
Shall be the joy of all the earth.

3 This is the Christ, our God and Lord,
Who in all need shall aid afford;

3. Translation by Catherine Winkworth (public domain).

That in His heavenly Kingdom blest
You may with us forever rest.

4 He brings those blessing, long ago
Prepared by God for all below,
Henceforth His Kingdom open stands
To you, as to the angel bands.

5 These are the tokens ye shall mark:
The swaddling-clothes and manger dark.
There ye shall find the young child laid
By whom the heavens and earth were made.

6 Now let us all with gladsome cheer,
Follow the shepherds, and draw near
To see the wondrous Gift of God,
Who hath His own dear Son bestowed.

7 Give heed, my heart, lift up thine eyes!
What is it in yon manger lies?
Who is this child, so young and fair?
Dear little Jesus lieth there.

8 Welcome to earth, Thou noble Guest,
Through whom the sinful world is blest!
Thou com'st to share my misery,
What thanks shall I return to Thee?

9 Ah! Lord, who hast created all,
How hast Thou made Thee weak and small,
That Thou must choose Thy infant bed,
Where humble cattle lately fed.

10 And were the world ten times as wide,
With gold and jewels beautified,
It would be far too small to be
A narrow cradle, Lord, for Thee.

11 For velvets soft and silken stuff
Thou hast but hay and straw so rough,
Whereon Thou, King, so rich and great,
As 'twere Thy heaven, art throned in state.

12 And thus, dear Lord, it pleased Thee
To make this truth quite plain to me,
That this world's honor, wealth and might,
Are naught and worthless in Thy sight.

13 Ah! dearest Jesus, holy Child,
Make Thee a bed, soft, undefiled,
Within my heart, that it may be
A quiet chamber kept for Thee.

14 My heart for very joy doth leap,
My lips no more can silence keep;
I, too, must sing with joyful tongue
That sweetest ancient cradle-song:

15 Glory to God in highest heaven,
Who unto man His Son hath given!
While angels sing with pious mirth
A glad New Year to all the earth.

"Dear Christians, One and All Rejoice"[4]

1 Dear Christians, one and all rejoice,
With exultation springing,
And, with united heart and voice
And holy rapture singing,
Proclaim the wonders God has done,
How His right arm the vict'ry won;
Right dearly it hath cost Him.

2 Fast bound in Satan's chains I lay;
Death brooded darkly o'er me.
Sin was my torment night and day;
In sin my mother bore me.
Deeper and deeper still I fell;
My life became a living hell,
So firmly sin possessed me.

---

4. Translation by Richard Massie (public domain).

3 My good works so imperfect were,
They had no power to aid me;
My will God's judgments could not bear,
Yea, prone to evil made me:
Grief drove me to despair, and I
Had nothing left me but to die;
To hell I fast was sinking.

4 Then God beheld my wretched state
With deep commiseration;
He thought upon His mercy great,
And willed my soul's salvation;
He turned to me a Father's heart;
Not small the cost! to heal my smart,
He gave His best and dearest.

5 He spoke to His beloved Son:
'Tis time to have compassion:
Then go, bright Jewel of my crown,
And bring to man salvation;
From sin and sorrow set him free;
Slay bitter death for him, that he
May live with Thee forever.

6 The Son obeyed right cheerfully,
And, born of virgin mother,
Came down upon the earth to me,
That He might be my brother:
His mighty power doth work unseen,
He came in fashion poor and mean,
And took the devil captive.

7 He sweetly said, "Hold fast by Me,
I am thy Rock and Castle.
Thy ransom I myself will be;
For thee I strive and wrestle:
For I am with thee, thou mine also;
And where I am, thou art; the foe
Shall never more divide us.

8 "For he shall shed my precious blood,
Me of my life bereaving;
All this I suffer for thy good,
Be steadfast and believing:
Life shall from death the vict'ry win,
My innocence shall bear thy sin,
So art thou blest forever.

9 "Now to My Father I depart,
From earth to heaven ascending,
Thence heavenly wisdom to impart,
The Holy Spirit sending:
He shall in trouble comfort thee,
Teach thee to know and follow me,
And to the truth conduct thee.

10 "What I have done and taught, do thou,
To do and teach endeavor;
So shall my kingdom flourish now,
And God be praised, forever:
Take heed lest men with base alloy
The heavenly treasure should destroy;
This counsel I bequeath thee."

"Christ Jesus Lay in Death's Strong Bands"[5]

1 Christ Jesus lay in death's strong bands,
for our offenses given;
but now at God's right hand He stands
and brings us life from heaven.
Therefore let us joyful be
and sing to God right thankfully
loud songs of hallelujah.
Hallelujah!

2 It was a strange and dreadful strife
when life and death contended;

5. Translation by Richard Massie (public domain).

the victory remained with life,
the reign of death was ended.
Holy Scripture plainly saith
that death is swallowed up by death;
its sting is lost forever.
Hallelujah!

3 Here the true Paschal Lamb we see,
whom God so freely gave us;
He died on the accursed tree—
so strong His love to save us.
See, His blood doth mark our door;
faith points to it, death passes o'er,
and Satan cannot harm us.
Hallelujah!

4 So let us keep the festival
whereto the Lord invites us;
Christ is Himself the Joy of all,
the Sun that warms and lights us.
By His grace He doth impart
eternal sunshine to the heart;
the night of sin is ended.
Hallelujah!

"Out of the Depths I Cry to You"[6]

1 Out of the depths I cry to Thee;
Lord, hear me, I implore Thee!
Bend down Thy gracious ear to me,
My prayer let come before Thee!
If Thou remember each misdeed,
If each should have its rightful meed,
Who may abide Thy presence?

2 Our pardon is Thy gift; Thy love
And grace alone avail us.

6. Translation by Catherine Winkworth (public domain).

Our works could ne'er our guilt remove,
The strictest life would fail us.
That none may boast himself of aught,
But own in fear Thy grace hath wrought
What in him seemeth righteous.

3 And thus, my hope is in the Lord,
And not in mine own merit;
I rest upon His faithful word
To them of contrite spirit.
That He is merciful and just,—
This is my comfort and my trust,
His help I wait with patience.

4 And though it tarry till the night
And round till morning waken,
My heart shall ne'er mistrust Thy might,
Nor count itself forsaken.
Do thus, O ye of Israel's seed,
Ye of the Spirit born indeed,
Wait for your God's appearing.

5 Though great our sins and sore our woes,
His grace much more aboundeth;
His helping love no limit knows,
Our utmost need it soundeth;
Our kind and faithful Shepherd He,
Who shall at last set Israel free
From all their sin and sorrow.

"Lord, Keep Us Steadfast in Your Word"[7]

1 Lord, keep us steadfast in your word;
curb those who by deceit or sword
would wrest the kingdom from your Son
and bring to naught all he has done.

7. Translation by Catherine Winkworth (public domain).

2 Lord Jesus Christ, your pow'r make known,
for you are Lord of lords alone;
defend your holy church, that we
may sing your praise eternally.

3 O Comforter of priceless worth,
send peace and unity on earth;
support us in our final strife
and lead us out of death to life.

Notes

Preface

1. There are many. Two in English translation are worth lifting up here: Oswald Bayer, *Martin Luther's Theology: A Contemporary Interpretation*, trans. Thomas H. Trapp (Grand Rapids: Eerdmans, 2007); and Bernhard Lohse, *Martin Luther's Theology: Its Historical and Systematic Development*, trans. Roy A. Harrisville (Minneapolis: Fortress, 1999). Even though these two works escape the worst excesses, purely "historical" introductions are often hermeneutically naive, especially in their alleged disinterestedness in aspiring to a pure representation of the past, when in reality the research is much influenced by the exigencies of German church history and intra-Lutheran polemics.

2. See, e.g., *Luther between Present and Past: Studies in Luther and Lutheranism*, ed. Ulrik Nissen, Anna Vind, Bo Holm, and Olli-Pekka Vainio (Helsinki: Luther-Agricola Society, 2004); and *Transformations in Luther's Theology: Historical and Contemporary Reflections*, ed. C. Helmer and B. K. Holm, Arbeiten zur Kirchen- und Theologiegeschichte 32 (Leipzig: Evangelische Verlagsanstalt, 2011).

Introduction

1. *The Oxford Encyclopedia of Martin Luther*, ed. Derek R. Nelson and Paul R. Hinlicky (New York: Oxford University Press, 2017).

2. See *The Oxford Handbook of Evangelical Theology*, ed. Gerald R. McDermott (New York: Oxford University Press, 2010); and Molly Worthen, *Apostles of Reason: The Crisis of Authority in American Evangelicalism* (New York: Oxford University Press, 2014).

Overture: "A Mighty Fortress Is Our God"

1. Volume 53 of *Luther's Works*, ed. Jaroslav Pelikan, Helmut T. Lehmann, and Christopher Boyd Brown, 75 vols. (Philadelphia: Muhlenberg and Fortress; St. Louis: Concordia, 1955–)—henceforth LW—contains translations and historical introductions

to Luther's hymns. The best and most current treatment of Luther's church music is Robin A. Leaver, *Luther's Liturgical Music: Principles and Implications* (Grand Rapids: Eerdmans, 2007).

2. Roy A. Harrisville, "The Life and Work of Ernst Käsemann (1906–1998)," *Lutheran Quarterly* 21, no. 3 (2007): 294–319.

3. See Ernst Käsemann, *Essays on New Testament Themes*, trans. W. J. Montague (London: SCM, 1971); and Käsemann, *New Testament Questions for Today*, trans. W. J. Montague (Philadelphia: Fortress, 1979).

Chapter 1 The New Birth

1. For the history of the composition and reception of this hymn, see Robin A. Leaver, *Luther's Liturgical Music: Principles and Implications* (Grand Rapids: Eerdmans, 2007), 135–41.

2. Karl Barth, *Church Dogmatics*, IV/4, *The Doctrine of Reconciliation*, trans. G. W. Bromiley and T. F. Torrance (Edinburgh: T&T Clark, 1974), 1–39; see further Paul R. Hinlicky, *Beloved Community: Critical Dogmatics after Christendom* (Grand Rapids: Eerdmans, 2015), 270–81.

3. LW 31:293–306.

4. See Brad S. Gregory, *The Unintended Reformation: How a Religious Revolution Secularized Society* (Cambridge, MA: Harvard University Press, 2012).

5. LW 35:365–80.

6. See, e.g., LW 35:371, 374, 376, 377.

7. LW 34:323–38.

8. LW 26–27.

9. Dietrich Bonhoeffer, *The Cost of Discipleship*, trans. R. H. Fuller (New York: Simon & Schuster, 1995). The affinity of this antinomianism with anti-Judaism, morphing into modern anti-Semitism, is not accidental and is a story I have told in my book *Before Auschwitz: What Christian Theology Must Learn from the Rise of Nazism* (Eugene, OR: Cascade, 2013).

10. LW 53:290–91.

11. So I have argued in Paul R. Hinlicky, *Paths Not Taken: Fates of Theology from Luther through Leibniz* (Grand Rapids: Eerdmans, 2010), which also lays out in detail the scholarly case for the difference between Luther and Melanchthon on justification described above.

12. Brad Gregory (*Unintended Reformation*, 100–101) has captured this devolution of "enthusiasm" to what Robert Bellah called contemporary "Sheilaism."

Chapter 2 The Bible

1. R. W. Meyer, *Leibniz and the Seventeenth-Century Revolution*, trans. J. P. Stern (Cambridge: Bowes and Bowes, 1952), 76.

2. Meyer, *Leibniz and the Seventeenth-Century Revolution*, 76.

3. Meyer, *Leibniz and the Seventeenth-Century Revolution*, 76.

4. LW 12:160–63.

5. R. Kendall Soulen, *The Divine Name(s) and the Holy Trinity*, vol. 1, *Distinguishing the Voices* (Louisville: Westminster John Knox, 2011), 238.

6. Paul R. Hinlicky, "Luther's Anti-Docetism in the *Disputatio de divinitate et humanitate Christi* (1540)," in *Creator Est Creatura: Luthers Christologie als Lehre*

von der Idiomenkommunikation, ed. O. Bayer and Benjamin Gleede (New York: de Gruyter, 2007), 139–85.

7. So Lutheran theologian Ted Peters, in *God—The World's Future: Systematic Theology for a New Era*, 3rd ed. (Minneapolis: Fortress, 2015), 679.

8. Janet Soskice, *Metaphor and Religious Language* (Oxford: Clarendon, 1987), 70.

9. Weimarer Ausgabe (henceforth WA) 35:423–25; LW 53:217–20. For the history of composition and reception, see Robin A. Leaver, *Luther's Liturgical Music: Principles and Implications* (Grand Rapids: Eerdmans, 2007), 161–72.

10. Oswald Bayer, *Martin Luther's Theology: A Contemporary Interpretation*, trans. Thomas H. Trapp (Grand Rapids: Eerdmans, 2007).

11. Christine Helmer, *The Trinity and Martin Luther: A Study on the Relationship between Genre, Language and the Trinity in Luther's Works, 1523–1546* (Mainz: Philipp von Zabern, 1999).

Chapter 3 Evangelization

1. LW 31:327–77.

2. Martin Luther, *The Bondage of the Will*, trans. J. I. Packer and O. R. Johnston (Grand Rapids: Revell, 2000), 315.

3. Luther, *Bondage of the Will*, 317 (trans. Packer and Johnston).

Chapter 4 The Atonement

1. LW 42.

2. Gerhard O. Forde, "The Work of Christ" (Seventh Locus), in *Christian Dogmatics*, ed. C. E. Braaten and R. W. Jenson, 2 vols. (Philadelphia: Fortress, 1984), 2:9.

3. WA 35:443–45; LW 53:255–57.

4. See George MacDonald's translation of this hymn in LW 53:257: "Jesus Christ, God's only Son . . . / from Death rending / Right and might, made him a jape."

5. WA 35:421–22; LW 53:221–24. For the history of the composition and reception of this hymn, see Robin A. Leaver, *Luther's Liturgical Music: Principles and Implications* (Grand Rapids: Eerdmans, 2007), 142–52.

Chapter 5 Catechesis as Christian Torah

1. *Catholic and Reformed: Selected Theological Writings of John Williamson Nevin*, ed. Charles Yrigoyen Jr. and George H. Bricker (Pittsburgh: Pickwick, 1978), 5.

2. Yrigoyen and Bricker, *Catholic and Reformed*, 6.

3. Yrigoyen and Bricker, *Catholic and Reformed*, 12 (emphasis in the original).

4. Scott H. Hendrix, *Recultivating the Vineyard: The Reformation Agendas of Christianization* (Louisville: Westminster John Knox, 2004).

5. *The Oxford Handbook of Evangelical Theology*, ed. Gerald R. McDermott (New York: Oxford University Press, 2010).

6. McDermott, *Oxford Handbook of Evangelical Theology*, 26.

7. McDermott, *Oxford Handbook of Evangelical Theology*, 40.

8. McDermott, *Oxford Handbook of Evangelical Theology*, 109.

9. McDermott, *Oxford Handbook of Evangelical Theology*, 28.

10. McDermott, *Oxford Handbook of Evangelical Theology*, 297, 302, 305.

11. McDermott, *Oxford Handbook of Evangelical Theology*, 253.

12. McDermott, *Oxford Handbook of Evangelical Theology*, 286.

13. McDermott, *Oxford Handbook of Evangelical Theology*, 204.

14. McDermott, *Oxford Handbook of Evangelical Theology*, 209–10.

15. On this contention, which underlies so much of Anglo-American Protestantism, see Don Thorsen, *Calvin vs. Wesley: Bringing Belief in Line with Practice* (Nashville: Abingdon, 2013).

16. See McDermott, *Oxford Handbook of Evangelical Theology*, 214.

17. McDermott, *Oxford Handbook of Evangelical Theology*, 216.

18. McDermott, *Oxford Handbook of Evangelical Theology*, 24, 241.

19. McDermott, *Oxford Handbook of Evangelical Theology*, 83, 88.

20. McDermott, *Oxford Handbook of Evangelical Theology*, 282–83, 320.

21. McDermott, *Oxford Handbook of Evangelical Theology*, 228.

22. McDermott, *Oxford Handbook of Evangelical Theology*, 227, 231.

23. McDermott, *Oxford Handbook of Evangelical Theology*, 307.

24. McDermott, *Oxford Handbook of Evangelical Theology*, 197–201.

25. Molly Worthen, *Apostles of Reason: The Crisis of Authority in American Evangelicalism* (New York: Oxford University Press, 2014), 20–21. Worthen goes on to show how, at every turning point in evangelical history in the twentieth century, the movement faltered on the conundrums attending inerrancy (see, e.g., 180, 187, 199, 207).

26. Christine Helmer, *Theology and the End of Doctrine* (Louisville: Westminster John Knox, 2014).

27. We will be following the contemporary translation edited by Robert Kolb and Timothy Wengert in *The Book of Concord: The Confessions of the Evangelical Lutheran Church* (Minneapolis: Fortress, 2000). Wengert, by the way, has published a helpful analysis, *Martin Luther's Catechisms: Forming the Faith* (Minneapolis: Fortress, 2009), which might be consulted for further study.

28. Ronald W. Roschke, "A Catechism of Luther's Catechisms," *Currents in Theology and Mission* 4, no. 2 (1977): 70; Dennis Ngien, "Theology and Practice of Prayer in Luther's Devotional and Catechetical Writings," *Luther-Bulletin* 14 (Fall 2005): 45.

29. Klaas Zwanepol, "The Structure and Dynamics of Luther's Catechism," *Acta Theologica* 31, no. 2 (2011): 408.

30. Roschke, "Catechism of Luther's Catechisms," 70–71.

Chapter 6 The Decalogue

1. *The Book of Concord: The Confessions of the Evangelical Lutheran Church*, ed. Robert Kolb and Timothy Wengert (Minneapolis: Fortress, 2000), 386–400.

2. No. 72 of "Radicalizing Reformation—Provoked by the Bible and Today's Crises: 94 Theses," http://www.radicalizing-reformation.com/index.php/en/theses .html.

3. *The Collected Works of Thomas Müntzer*, ed. Peter Matheson (Edinburgh: T&T Clark, 1988), 251.

4. See, further, Paul R. Hinlicky, *Divine Complexity: The Rise of Creedal Christianity* (Minneapolis: Fortress, 2011), 167–73.

5. Arthur H. Drevlow, "The History, Significance, and Application of Luther's Catechisms," *Concordia Journal* 5, no. 5 (September 1979): 174.

6. See website in note 2 above.

7. See, further, Paul R. Hinlicky, *Beloved Community: Critical Dogmatics after Christendom* (Grand Rapids: Eerdmans, 2015).

8. James Arne Nestigen, "The Lord's Prayer in Luther's Catechism," *Word & World* 22, no. 1 (Winter 2002): 39. This article, incidentally, provides good scholarly bibliography for further study.

9. John Witte Jr., *Law and Protestantism: The Legal Teachings of the Lutheran Reformation* (Cambridge: Cambridge University Press, 2002).

10. See, further, Klaas Zwanepol, "The Structure and Dynamics of Luther's Catechism," *Acta Theologica* 31, no. 2 (2011): 399–400.

11. Oswald Bayer, *Martin Luther's Theology: A Contemporary Interpretation*, trans. Thomas H. Trapp (Grand Rapids: Eerdmans, 2007).

12. Giorgio Agamben, *Homo Sacer: Sovereign Power and Bare Life*, trans. D. Heller-Roazen (Stanford, CA: Stanford University Press, 1998).

13. Steven Ozment, *When Fathers Ruled: Family Life in Reformation Europe* (Cambridge, MA: Harvard University Press, 1983).

14. See Christopher Lasch, *Haven in a Heartless World: The Family Besieged* (New York: Basic Books, 1977).

Chapter 7 The Creed

1. *The Book of Concord: The Confessions of the Evangelical Lutheran Church*, ed. Robert Kolb and Timothy Wengert (Minneapolis: Fortress, 2000), 431–40.

2. Paul R. Hinlicky, *Divine Complexity: The Rise of Creedal Christianity* (Minneapolis: Fortress, 2011), 137–58.

3. Dietrich Bonhoeffer, *Ethics*, trans. N. H. Smith (New York: MacMillan, 1978), 196–207. In *Bonhoeffer's Reception of Luther* (Oxford: Oxford University Press, 2017), 77–102, Michael P. DeJong has set the record straight for both Luther and Bonhoeffer on this much disputed and convoluted matter.

4. Klaas Zwanepol, "The Structure and Dynamics of Luther's Catechism," *Acta Theologica* 31, no. 2 (2011): 404.

Chapter 8 The Christian Life

1. *The Book of Concord: The Confessions of the Evangelical Lutheran Church*, ed. Robert Kolb and Timothy Wengert (Minneapolis: Fortress, 2000), 440–56.

2. Klaas Zwanepol, "The Structure and Dynamics of Luther's Catechism," *Acta Theologica* 31, no. 2 (2011): 402; Dennis Ngien, "Theology and Practice of Prayer in Luther's Devotional and Catechetical Writings," *Luther-Bulletin* 14 (Fall 2005): 45, 66.

3. On this see Zwanepol, "Structure and Dynamics of Luther's Catechism," 400.

4. James Arne Nestigen, "The Lord's Prayer in Luther's Catechism," *Word & World* 22, no. 1 (Winter 2002): 42.

5. Nestigen, "Lord's Prayer in Luther's Catechism," 43.

6. See Kolb and Wengert, *Book of Concord*, 456–67.

7. See his lament about this in the Baptismal Booklet in the Small Catechism (Kolb and Wengert, *Book of Concord*, 371–75).

8. See Kolb and Wengert, *Book of Concord*, 467–76.

9. Ignatius, *To the Smyrnaeans* 6, in *The Apostolic Fathers: Greek Texts and English Translations*, ed. and trans. Michael W. Holmes, 3rd ed. (Grand Rapids: Baker Academic, 2007), 253, 255.

10. See Kolb and Wengert, *Book of Concord*, 476–80.

Postlude

1. WA 35:467; LW 53:304–5. For the history and composition of this hymn, see Robin A. Leaver, *Luther's Liturgical Music: Principles and Implications* (Grand Rapids: Eerdmans, 2007), 107–15.

2. For the detailed argument in these connections, see Paul R. Hinlicky, "Luther in Marx," in *The Oxford Encyclopedia of Martin Luther*, ed. Derek R. Nelson and Paul R. Hinlicky (New York: Oxford University Press, 2017).

3. LW 31:92.

4. LW 46.

5. See Michael P. DeJonge, *Bonhoeffer's Reception of Luther* (Oxford: Oxford University Press, 2017).

6. LW 53:267.

7. On this tangled knot of questions, see Paul R. Hinlicky, *Luther vs. Pope Leo: A Conversation in Purgatory* (Nashville: Abingdon, 2017).

8. With reservations, see Rod Dreher, *The Benedict Option: A Strategy for Christians in a Post-Christian Nation* (New York: Sentinel, 2017).

Index of Names and Subjects

Printed and bound by CPI Group (UK) Ltd, Croydon, CR0 4YY

13/04/2025

14656457-0003